D1637829

TWO OLD FARTS AND A MOTORHOME!!

PATTI TRICKETT

authorHOUSE®

AuthorHouse™
1663 Liberty Drive
Bloomington, IN 47403
www.authorhouse.com
Phone: 1-800-839-8640

© 2012 by Patti Trickett. All rights reserved.

No part of this book may be reproduced, stored in a retrieval system, or transmitted by any means without the written permission of the author.

First published by AuthorHouse   01/17/2012

ISBN: 978-1-4678-8314-6 (sc)
ISBN: 978-1-4678-8315-3 (hc)
ISBN: 978-1-4678-8316-0 (ebk)

Printed in the United States of America

Any people depicted in stock imagery provided by Thinkstock are models, and such images are being used for illustrative purposes only.
Certain stock imagery © Thinkstock.

Because of the dynamic nature of the Internet, any web addresses or links contained in this book may have changed since publication and may no longer be valid. The views expressed in this work are solely those of the author and do not necessarily reflect the views of the publisher, and the publisher hereby disclaims any responsibility for them.

CONTENTS

DEDICATED TO MY HUSBAND GEORGE CHRISTOPHER

WHOSE CONSTANT ENCOURAGEMENT AND LOVE HAS BEEN

INSTRUMENTAL IN WRITING THIS BOOK.

ABOVE ALL, DO NOT LOSE YOUR DESIRE TO WALK. EVERY DAY, I WALK MYSELF INTO A STATE OF WELL BEING; AND WALK AWAY FROM EVERY ILLNESS.

I HAVE WALKED MYSELF INTO MY BEST THOUGHTS, AND KNOW OF NO THOUGHT SO BURDENSOME; THAT ONE CANNOT WALK AWAY FROM IT.

BUDDHA.

CHAPTER 1

RENTING AND BUYING A MOTOR HOME, AND OUR SCOTTISH HOLIDAY.

Where do I start, I think I will start at the end! The end of our working life as such. Up until now we have both run a very busy food business in a well known seaside area for just over 23 years. Our thoughts, actions and lives were literally centred around the shop, staff and customers; slotting in our entertainment whenever we could.

We both love walking and the outdoor life, taking our motor home to the Lake District or the Yorkshire Dales whenever we found time for ourselves, parking the van in some out of the way place and walking 'off map'. Our greatest pleasure was to do a circular walk with spectacular views of the hills and dales and end up at the local public house at the end of the day. There is nothing nicer than to lift the latch of an old oak beamed pub, where the very warmth of a blazing open fire hits you after being out in the cold for a few hours. Find a cosy corner and sit with your favourite tipple and maybe play dominoes or chat about the day and relive the events which had taken place.

These weekends away and the odd full week's holiday have continued for a few years, in so much as I knew what to expect in coming home after a day's walking to climb back into our car and return home, or stay with friends at their house over night, when we had walked with them that day. Or ideally, book into a pretty bed and breakfast accommodation and have a piping hot shower and a warm and cosy bed to sleep in, and have the added luxury of a delicious full English breakfast before we departed next morning.

It all started quite by accident, a series of events which took place, call it fate if you will, but the ball started rolling and I stood, as a spectator, mouth agape.

May I briefly take you back 4 years to a time when we had neither our motor home nor our little place in Crete. My husband had "always fancied having a motor home". Next thing I know, we are visiting showrooms and exhibitions to study various makes, models and interiors and getting more and more confused by the minute.

"I know" I said one evening, "let's hire a motor home, and that way we can try it out and see if we would really like to buy one".

Talking it over for a few days, we both agreed that it would be the best thing to do. So arrangements were made to drive up to Scotland and collect a new hire van from a small family run business situated on the North East side of Scotland.

"Why hire one way down here in the North West of England, when we can clog it up the motorway in our car and get there in half the time" my husband said. So the deal was done and we set off in earnest for our new adventure in Scotland. I might point out at this stage that we didn't know one end of a motor home from another, so all the knobs and switches were totally alien to us. The good thing is that my husband is a very good driver, having driven large vehicles in his line of business.

After a pleasant journey up to Scotland and taking receipt of the motor home, we were relieved to find that it wasn't hard learning what all the knobs and switches were for. So this was the start of our new experiences in a motor home.

Our first night in the rental van proved to be a 'scream'—quite literally!! As I have already pointed out, we are on virgin territory regarding the mysterious acts of camping and caravanning. With the careful instructions that we got from the owners plus, reading the thick manual on 'how to' we managed to set the van up to comfort level. Hooked up on the electric on the site, fresh water in the tanks for later, we had a lovely meal with wine and sat reading until bedtime.

We hired a 5 berth motor home, so we would have the choice of climbing the ladder to bed and sleeping over the cab, or re-assembling the sitting area into a low double bed—the choice was ours!! I must point out that at this moment in time, when looking at motor homes and caravans, no one tells you that bare feet and wooden ladders combined, are not suitable bedfellows!! And with that in mind, our first night was a painful experience, as one does not wear slippers in bed!

Oh! Yes! I hear you say. Why not wear the slippers up the ladder to bed—and THEN take them off!! Well, actually, I did, only thing is—if you get 'caught short' in the middle of the night, and want to use the loo; only to find your slippers have gone 'walk about' somewhere in the bed!! And that is exactly what happened!!

Not just that, I am afraid!—But climbing a ladder does not come natural to me, as I am frightened of heights etc. Plus, when I laid flat and looked up at the ceiling, unfortunately it was only a short distance from my face and felt like I was in a coffin. I am claustrophobic too!

"Oh! I don't like this. I feel like I am in a coffin".

With that, he said "Turn on your side and go to sleep; you won't see anything when I put the lights off".

Sitting bolt upright in bed, and banging my head on the ceiling, I shouted "Ouch" in a loud voice. "What do you mean? I am frightened of the dark, you know I am".

His patience started slipping then, but all the same, gave me an indulgent and watery smile. "Just go to sleep dear". Knowing him as well as I do, that meant;

"Don't push it dear, or shut up you phobic woman!!

So I did!!

He lay down next to me and was just dozing off to sleep, when panic started rising in my chest and throat as the light went off and we were plunged into total darkness. Before I could stop myself, fear bubbled up into my throat and then . . . .

'OH! Put the light on quickly' I shrieked at the top of my voice. The poor man sat up so fast, I estimated: 0-60 mph - also banging his 'something or other' at the same time on the ceiling and trying desperately to find the light switch.

"Oh! Be quiet, you will have the entire site awake and they will think I am murdering you". (And I will if you don't shut up!!) Ha Ha!! . . . No, he didn't say the last bit, but probably thought it all the same.

After he calmed me down with promises and reassuring words, he made a cup of herbal tea. We tried once more to go to bed; it was very late by then and total silence in the grounds of the park.

Helping me up the little wooden ladder, slippers on after hunting for them under the duvet. He told me that if he left a small light on, would that be any better?

I said 'it would', and we settled down for the night.

As I mentioned earlier, you get to a certain age in life, and one cannot sleep right through the night without getting a 'call of nature'. I must have been about 3 a.m. when I woke with an urge to use the bathroom. By then, my darling husband was in the land of nod, making a noise like a traction engine in full tilt! As I was on the inside of the double bed next to the wall, I could neither move or get up and climb over him without disturbing his sleep! Even if I could have negotiated the dreaded ladder, which was highly unlikely with my track record. My slippers had gone 'walk about' AGAIN!! And after carefully turning down towards the bottom of the bed like a snail, and groping my way around, I finally gave up on that idea. I was in a dilemma as to what to do.

Well, my friends, what do you think I did? Yes!—got it in one!!

'Chris, Chris, are you awake love?' No reply! (Louder, as he is a

'Chris, Chris, Oh! CHRIS, I NEED the bathroom.'

There was a groan, then some grunting and moaning coming from deep within the duvet. With that, the duvet got kicked off, and with arms flailing, he was trying to get up without banging his 'something or other' again! My poor bleary eyed husband slowly climbed down the ladder waiting patiently at the bottom to give me instruction and negotiation as he encouraged me to get to the edge of the bed.

Slowly swiveling round, I gingerly put my now slippered foot on the first rung.

May I freeze frame this picture for you to create yet another one at this stage!

My husband has always slept in the 'all together', and that night was no exception.

I, on the other hand, have always worn a nightgown, so as I was coming down the ladder yelping, my husband had placed both hands on my bottom to help steer me down, and at the same time encouraging me with comforting words so I didn't start panicking again and make familiar shrieking noises.

Safely down, the poor man had to stand and wait until I had finished in the bathroom, so as to help me back up the ladder again and into bed.

Needless to say over breakfast next morning we both agreed that we would have to use the other bed facility that night and sleep nearer to the floor.

Before getting ready for bed that night we both thought it would be wise to make the bed up first before getting undressed.

"It cannot be so difficult, plenty of people do it regularly" my husband said. So out came the seat cushions, and the wooden slats were re-assembled into place. Then the cushion seating went back on again to form the mattress, making the bed flat and low to the floor.

"All well and good" you say?

Well yes and no, because now the double bed had priority down the middle of the floor of the van, and there was literally no room to get access to the stove top or over to the other side. So we went to bed at 8-00 p.m. My husband declaring that he could catch up on his missed sleep 'from last night's fracas'. I slept okay, I guess, if you like sleeping almost on the floor in a draft with your nose pressed up against the bottom of the oven door. But at least I didn't get into another panic and start screaming again.

Next morning a yawn and a stretch, "whose making a cuppa" no reply—"I said, whose" . . . .my voice trailed off. Chris as on his hands and knees (not a pretty sight first thing in the morning, after what I have just told you). He said, "We will both have to get up before coffee, as I cannot get to the stove top to put the kettle on, there isn't enough room".

So that was how it was for 2 weeks, no cuppa in bed for us and an extra cuddle down. It was 'up and at 'em' for a fortnight! Despite that, we had the most wonderful and adventurous holiday, seeing new places and experiencing new things every day. Vowing that when we returned home after our holiday, we would step up the intensity of looking for our own motor home.

We wanted to cut across country to the pretty West side of Scotland via Callender, Dunoon and Loch Lomond in the Trossachs National Park; and then onward to the quaint and lovely seaside village of Oban which we eventually did. But we lingered on the banks of Loch Lomond with the irresistible 'Three Lochs Drive', which was very memorable to us. As I recall, it was a warm sultry day (unusual for Scotland). By the time 4-00 p.m. came we were looking for somewhere to pull up and rest for the night. We followed the road sign which indicated the Lochs Drive, as curiosity had prompted us to take a look.

There before us was the most beautiful loch stretching out into the distance. The sun was still quite high in the sky, so that the reflections of the overhanging trees around the loch were casting reflections into the deep dark green waters, to create a double reflective picture. The surrounding areas were covered in lush green pine forests making the loch itself like a 'jewel in the crown'. We both remarked that we couldn't leave this straight away and decided to camp there for the night. We found a lovely flat area in which to park the van right up to the water's edge, and as we watched several day trippers going back home, we felt very happy that we would be the only ones there that night.

Unpacking the folding outdoor chairs and bringing the little table out of our motor home, we sat at the loch side to have a drink and enjoy the remains of the day. The sunsets in Scotland are something to behold, as it was sinking slowly behind the green vista of pine trees; every now and then we would hear a fish plopping back down into the still waters of the loch as it had briefly come up for air. We were at peace with the world, and gave a deep sigh and nodded our approval to each other.

After a very restful night's sleep, we were up with the lark next morning, and having our separate jobs to do, we enjoyed a hearty breakfast of bacon and eggs.

We meandered further on toward Oban taking our time to enjoy the lovely scenery as we drove. Getting to Oban town early afternoon, we parked up and had a walk to stretch our legs before motoring up to the camp site North of Oban and stop to rest for the night. We hooked up in a sheltered area of the site with the lovely views out towards the Island of Carrera. The sunset ran true to form, as it looked like the sky was on fire, with a spectrum of deep reds, blues and purple lighting up the whole sky. Maybe a giant artist had come with a brush and painted it all??

Sleeping deeply and in total comfort and relaxation, we woke to another beautiful dry and sunny morning determined that today would be the day we would travel over by the little ferry at the top of the road to the Island of Carrera which is well known for its bird and wildlife. The little Island of Carrera is situated in the Firth of

Lorne, and regular ferries run from Oban to the popular Isles of Mull, Colonssay, and Jura. Islay is interlinked to the seaside town of Tarbet further down the coastline. We did not know however, that one has to turn the sign around by the ferry point to hail the little boat, and then the ferry master knows that someone wants to be picked up and brought over to Carrera.

After standing there for a few minutes, a local guy told us, "You must turn this board around so that the ferry man can see that you want to be picked up and brought across, and that you must do this on the return journey from Carrera if he is over on the mainland".

We thought that this was really cute and didn't think that kind of thing happened any more. Alighting from the little ferry boat later, we set off with great enthusiasm for our forthcoming walk round the Island and to enjoy the warm sunshine. Suitably dressed for walking, sensible boots, waterproofs incase the weather turned for the worst. Rucksack loaded with water and a light picnic, compass tucked into my husband's pocket, he never goes walking without it; we set off to do the complete circular walk before it went dark. We were previously informed that the island was rich in bird and wildlife, and very popular with summer tourists. Half an hour into the walk we saw something which made us feel very sad. There must have been an outbreak of mixamitosis with the rabbits on the island, as one or two of them stumbled across us, blind and dying with the lack of food!

The views were breathtaking as we headed towards the castle remains along the edge of the high cliff tops. We decided to take a closer look and include it in our walk. We believe that they have bred cattle on the island for many years, on maturity; they are encouraged to swim over to the mainland and then be sold on at auction. We didn't have the privilege of seeing this first hand, but agreed that it must have been an unusual sight, imagining them doing the exact thing hundreds of years ago when the world was a very different place. Half way round we stopped to have a rest and a picnic. We always enjoy eating outside, and a good walk certainly sharpens your appetite! Gazing across at the calm blue sea surrounding the island and feeling the warmth of the day, with a soft wind to ruffle our hair. Can walking get any better than this we asked ourselves?

We deviated to the ruins of the castle after our brief sojourn. Running up the undulating incline towards the castle, I shouted back to Chris, "How proud and majestic the castle looks still after all these years".

One can see in mind's eye the battles taking place centuries before, and the castle 'keep' under constant threat from the enemy. Who built it? Where did they get the stone from? Did they bring it from the mainland? If so, how did they? In a boat? What kind of strong boat would carry heavy stone? How long would it take to build it? And what about weather conditions etc. The list goes on and on, and we are in constant conversation when we are out walking, not experts, but curious and very interested all the same. We usually try to make up a resulting story on what little knowledge we have learnt in the past and then fill the details in when we get back home and use the computer. It is fun trying and we think knowledge 'is all'.

Finishing the walk, and already it was teatime. We turned the old wooden sign around again to call the ferry man over as he was temporarily residing over on the Oban side waiting for his next instruction. Back at the van, we decided to move on the next day, so much to see and do, and loving the freedom and last minute decisions we can bring about on a mere whim of fancy. Pouring over our map of Scotland after a delicious dinner, we decided we wanted to continue up the lovely West side and maybe go right over the very top of Scotland if the weather continued to be in our favour, with good clear visibility. Anyone who has ventured up to the Highlands know full well that once the weather breaks, you may as well put a sack over your head, because that is precisely what you will see—NOTHING!!

The other hindrance which springs to mind is the dreaded mosquitoes!! They don't just have them abroad, they are alive and kicking in the Highlands of Scotland, and they really hurt when they take careful aim at your arms and legs. Usually found by still waters, such as the lochs. I got bitten one day when we camped by one of the beautiful lochs and sat outside in the early evening. Jumping up quickly, I rushed off into the van to get some repellent. My husband swears by citronella lamp oil! And like Henry Cooper, he 'splashes it on all over'.

He says he would rather smell of lamp oil than get the allergic reaction once they have bitten him.

Travelling still further North past the beautiful little town of Fort William at the very edge of Loch Linnhe, we continue up making a left deviation towards the Kyle of Lochalsh and stop over to take in the natural loveliness of it all.

"Its times like this," I said to my husband, hand in hand and gazing into the distance, "that you really believe in God, the maker of all things beautiful".

Gasping in awe and shaking our heads in the magnificent beauty of each place we travel, we will say "can the next place be even more breathtaking than what we see right now?"

Then around the next bend or over the next hill, we would find even more loveliness of wild stunning beauty. The dramatic colours of the rugged hills and rocks as we drove along, the deep blues and greens in the fathomless waters of the broody lochs, constant movement of the waters depending on the climatic changes and time of year. The sun coming through the heavily planted pine forests stretching for miles along the roadside with occasional 'breaks' every so often purposely done by the Forestry Commission to help in containment of forest fires. Semi darkness under the dense plantation caught my eye as we cruised along. "Nothing seems to grow right underneath the pine trees" I remarked. "No greenery or shrubs—nothing!!"

"It's too dark, that is why Patti. As it is, some of the pine trees are trying to grow up through the dense canopy of other trees, searching for light, he replied.

Shy and reclusive deer grazed in some small clearings waiting for a predator to spook them, so that they dart off at an amazing speed back into their dark and gloomy hideaway out of danger. Elegant and graceful heads tilted, sniffing the air for imminent signs of danger, brown eyes firmly fixed, wary and watching whilst bending their beautiful elegant necks to nibble at juicy grasses or lichen.

"You can see where the Scottish people got their original inspirations for the tartans" I said softly to Chris, as we drove along. "I believe the tartan is the very essence of what we are witnessing here today. The many tarns, hills and lochs, the light and shade, the ever changing colours of the beautiful lochs. The four seasons which change the colours of leaves on the trees in the Highlands. It's all here! And it's all there! In the colourful tartans they wear with pride.

Driving into the coastal town of Ullapool next evening, we find the most delightful site directly overlooking the sea. The owner of the site, a really friendly American guy made us most welcome and after formalities, directed us to our pitch, our motor home faced directly out to sea with fabulous views. We got settled in and decided that we would stay here for 2 days, rest and look around and maybe do a good walk either 'off map' or a well known walk which most site owners will tell you about. Whilst I started on the evening meal, Chris put the electric on and filled the tank up with fresh water for later. Coming together after an hour or so, we sat and watched the magnificent sun setting over the sea, the usual deep myriad of colours and spoke of how much we had enjoyed another exciting fun filled day in our motor home.

After a hearty breakfast next morning, we donned our walking boots and a warm jumper in case it turned colder, striding out along the narrow coastal path. We had heard from the friendly American site owner that there were basking seals just a few miles out to sea. "Look carefully, he said; you will be sure to see them". It was another dry and bright day with good visibility so we strode out in eager anticipation. After a while, we stopped for a rest and sat on a well placed bench to have a drink of water which we had brought with us in the rucksack. We both sat quietly, staring intently, concentrating on any movement in the calm waters of The Minch. Presently, our patience was rewarded, as first one little nose and a half submerged head popped up to take a breath, then another, and another; until we could see half a dozen seals quizzically looking about them.

"Oh! Goodness me, I said excitedly, jumping up and down, they are over there". "Oh! Aren't they lovely? Tugging at Chris' arm. "Do you think they can see us?

"Doubt it, Chris replied quietly staring out towards the frolicking seals, "but you never know, they just might".

I think in hindsight, they were too far away for them to pay us any attention, but we sat on the bench for some time anyway, watching them, spellbound and unblinking at their naturally graceful movements in the water. It was the first time for both of us to see wild seals in their natural environment, it was a remarkable sight!

"It must be like this when tourists go abroad and see a school of whales in their home environment, I said, just as thrilling!!

Getting back in the early evening, we decided that as it was our Wedding Anniversary this day, being 16th June. We would get showered and changed in the neat and clean toilet block on the site and go into Ullapool town for an evening meal and sample the local cuisine. It was our lucky day that day, because when we arrived shortly before 7-00 p.m. a crowd had gathered around the narrow main street. With posters on the shop windows, and general chat amongst the other tourists who were waiting patiently, it was regarding the local children who would be coming down shortly to dance and play the bagpipes in the square as a local 'gathering'. We later found out that it was the Ullapool under 15 year old pipe band and dancers, who started as young as 5 years old!

We could hear them before we could see them and it reminded us of the legend of the Scottish Pipers in the wars down through the ages, coming over the purple heather strewn brow of the rugged windblown hills in the Highlands. Through the early morning mists, colourful tartan kilts swaying to the time of the haunting strains of the bagpipes. Advancing on their enemy to do battle. What a frightening sight that must have been for the enemy!! So here they came again, advancing down the cobbled street like their forefathers had done. Not frightening now, but it made you shiver with THEIR PRIDE as they marched in time down to the little square below. How lovely they all looked! Young boys not yet in their prime, but fiercely proud of who they were and where they were born. Large crowds gathered around them to form a circle when they eventually reached the square. In the attentive crowd there were many local folk, husbands and wives, children on their own or with friends and family. Visitors like ourselves, curious as to what they may see, waiting and watching for the entertainment to begin.

Presently, and without too much hurry, they formed straight lines, four abreast. Two rows of pipers, making 8 pipers in all. Next came the big bass drum, handled by a young man not much bigger than the impressive drum he held; and in his hands were two twirling sticks with large pom poms at each end to beat in time to the music. Then another two rows of children playing the side drums balanced carefully on one side of the hip, those were the rat-a-tat-tat sound giving a musical dimension to the music. Following on came the brass section, making a total of around 20 children in this impressive local band. As they stood shoulder to shoulder in preparation, we noticed the various colourful tartans of their ancestor's clan. Some red, some blue, and some green tartan; all worn with pride and handed down through the generations by their forefathers.

Once the 'gathering' was under way, and watching them in total admiration as they smartly marched up and down the square; turning together at one end of the concreted yard to advance again to the haunting strains of the pipes and drums. One young lady about 12 years old came marching past us, heaving her side drum as she walked. It was a 'one step, two step, and then hitch the drum up on her third step.' Poor girl, she must have been struggling to carry such a heavy instrument.

The pipe major stood out in both our minds in the following weeks, long after we had left Scotland, and returned home again. We both had commented on how well trained he was to give the command and lead the others, himself still being of tender years. His stature and very presence was so authoritative, with his shock of bright red hair and freckles, the stern but understanding way he commanded his eager troupe was a credit to him and sheer delight to us. The pipers took it in turns to play a solo piece and listening to a lively reel or a mournful ballad, it was very entertaining and well played. Not a missed note or mistake was made; they must have practiced for hours to get it to perfection.

Then it was the turn of the young dancers, children as young as 5 years old doing the very difficult and intricate sword dance took the centre stage. Nimble on their toes, leaping high into the air, in perfect rhythm to the haunting strains of the bagpipes. Arms and hands positioned as 'stags horns' to complete their pose. Enthusiastic and appreciative applause followed each display, with short breaks in between for the pipers and dancers to rest and regroup. The two hour display flew quickly by and our favourite 'Rob Roy' gently but firmly re-assembled the talented little troupe to march them back over the brow of the hill and away home again!!

Silence, and anti-climax prevailed and everyone turned as if in confusion as to what to do next! What now, you could see on the faces of the crowd near us. Until thoughts were gathered and sensibilities returned once more.

"I know, let's walk further along the village high street and eat now, Chris remarked. "I am starving after all that pipe blowing and jigging up and down in the square".

"Oh yes! I said laughing, I could well see you participating in the Highland dancing and marching with the pipers wearing a kilt; with your hairy legs, you would get arrested".

"Come on then, I am hungry too".

Walking along the narrow pavements past the little old fashioned shops, with their low doorways and steep roof to protect against the snow and heavy rain in the bleak winters of Scotland, we saw a welcoming, and well lit public house serving delicious homemade food which we had noticed earlier in the day. Hearing familiar strains of lively Scottish folk music coming from within, it enticed us to take a closer look. As we got a bit nearer to the inn, there was the sound of laughter and clapping as a particular piece of music came to an end. Lifting the latch on the old and weather beaten door we entered, stooping low to avoid 'duck or grouse' to find a pleasant trio of musicians playing in the corner of the room. The pretty middle aged woman played the squeezebox, a good looking dark haired man played on rhythm guitar. A distinguished elderly guy played the hand held small flat drum, with a double cover ended stick, he would beat alternate ends in time to the music.

They all took their turns in singing, the woman had a very sweet voice which rose and fell with some of the old traditional ballads. They sang and played almost all of the time we were there, encouraged on by the appreciative audience who sat in a semicircle around them, sending a drink over now and then as a reward for the entertainment.

Chris found us a cosy corner with a soft and well upholstered bench to sit and eat our dinner. It was by the 'jam jar' glass bow fronted window—well lit by lamp light which gave a warm glow around the room. We could hear the lovely music coming from the other room, with some folk joining in the chorus. Other people on an evening out were sitting quite near us, and were busily tucking into the evening meal which looked delicious! The interior of the room was furnished in a very old style, with an oak beamed ceiling and plush fabrics in a warm burgundy colour, lending a lot of character to a public house which was built many years ago. Horse brasses and old pictures of the village and surrounding areas were hung on the bumpy uneven walls. Behind the dark wood, but well lit bar were more whiskies than we have ever seen in our lives. Beer and lager were evident but not really in view. As beer was the same price as a whisky! My husband eventually chose one just because he liked the look of the label on the bottle! Not being whisky drinkers either one of us, we had not the experience of what we liked or not.

"I don't think I will bother with one after all," I said, replacing Chris' whisky on the table after having a sip. "It tastes like a nasty medicine to me, so I won't do it justice".

Chris found his whisky to be so smooth, and so nice, he ordered another one later in the evening.

We ordered our dinner, and when it came, it was served to us in very large soup bowls, filled to brimming with the most delicious and piping hot food. We had both ordered roast shank of local Scottish lamb with fresh, local vegetables and a very large baked potato each! It really did fill the 'gap' and we both felt totally replete when the bowls were eventually wiped clean with warm homemade bread. We were then offered the 'sweet menu' but declined, although it looked delicious as well, we couldn't eat another mouthful.

The musicians played on and on and the place got noisier and noisier as folk started singing to the ballads and songs they knew, fuelled by good old Scottish whisky! Feet tapping and hands clapping in time to a lively reel, we joined in with everyone; it was such a good atmosphere and a brilliant evening.

Chris said "it's getting late now Patti and it's time to go".

Walking back down the narrow pavement once more, dimly lit, we shone our narrow beamed torch back to the motor home. Arm in arm, laughing and talking about the night's event; we both said how lovely our Anniversary had been and how memorable it was. We slept like new born babies and woke refreshed to yet another bright and sunny day to look forward to what adventures lay ahead.

Leaving Ullapool, and its friendly people behind us, we headed still further North towards Cape Wrath and the very top of the beautiful and rugged Highlands. We continued with the warm settled weather which gave way to magnificent views as we drove along. We stopped for a light lunch in the van on the Durness road, looking out to the deep blue waters and beyond. To our right we could just make out the Orkney Islands in the distance, where, we were told by another couple who had just returned from camping on one of the islands that the archaeology was not to be missed. I told them that I was really interested in the 'land clearances' having just read a book about it before coming away on holiday. It was very sad to hear how whole communities were broken up and virtually destroyed by rich landowners who wanted to reclaim their lands back. These poor people were left to their own devices to survive or starve by the roadside. A lot did starve to death before reaching the large ships to take them to the 'new lands' of Australia, Canada or America in the hope of building a new life there.

The Orkney Islands became a lot clearer as we travelled along towards Thurso for our night stop. Soft, undulating landscapes gave way to the harsh and rugged terrain now and looking at the local characters we saw in the small towns and village hamlets as we drove by, we commented on how hard it must be for them to live right up here and how much it was etched on their craggy faces which stretched back generations because of it.

We didn't go to John O'Groats, because everyone does, and we thought it would be too commercial and disappointing to do so. Instead, we made our way slowly back down the Eastern coastline on the A99, and then the A9 to Dingwall, where one cloudy but dry afternoon, we got talking to a lovely lady who ran a small inn. We spent a couple of hours in her company, sat in front of a roaring log fire talking about our respective families. Early evening and with dusk falling, we headed slowly back to our little home on wheels. We have become much attached to the van now as it has been instrumental in providing us with many lovely holidays and adventures. Settling down for the evening after supper, we planned our travel route for the next day.

Climbing steadily down now towards Perth, where we had left our car for 2 weeks with the owners of the rental motor home. We stayed on the A9 and travelled through the centre of the very beautiful Cairngorms National Park where we would spend the last 2 days of our holiday. Donning walking boots and suitable outer clothing once more, we walked under the dark green canopy of the damp scented pine trees. The forest floor was barren of any significant shrub growth as before, just now and then where there had been a break in the dense forest of trees, a few ferns and toadstools had grown spasmodically. Far in the distance, as a backdrop, the magnificent and dramatic Cairngorm Mountains were standing as silent sentinels, there forever for thousands of years. Ever changing colours and hews in the periodic sunshine and the ever strong Northern winds blowing the scudding clouds across the pale blue skies.

FOREVER THE WINDS BLOW.
FOREVER THE WATERS MOVE.
NOT FOR ONE MOMENT, SINCE TIME BEGAN—
HAVE THEY BEEN STILL!!!

We were in Scotland touring for 2 weeks. Sometimes on pretty campsites with all the facilities, sometimes, when we were in such a remote place 'wild camping' for a couple of nights until we felt the need to empty our disposable toilet in the motor home, and have a shower, and then to fill our tank up with fresh drinking water. I remember one occasion when we had camped by a loch right in the middle of nowhere. I had bought a plastic collapsible water carrier with me, and eager to use it I said to Chris, that I would go down to the loch with my carrier and get some fresh loch water to boil for a drink.

"You don't need to do that Patti, he said, we have enough fresh water in the tank and we have already filled up the 6 plastic water bottles before we set off from the last site".

Ignoring him, I picked up my carrier, and carefully walked down to the water's edge. It was quite shallow by my sandaled feet, and as the water was crystal clear, you could see the bottom where some tiny stones and debris lay. I was so excited as to be privileged to be able to do this; I forgot to take my sandals off and proceeded into the deeper water beyond.

"Look, I said to my husband, as I had carefully carried my yellow water carrier back to the van, I have managed to get a full bucket of lovely clear loch water for a drink later".

"Looking me up and down, his eyes landed on my very wet feet and dripping sandals, he said in a quiet voice. "That's very good Patti, but look at your sandals".

"Oh! They'll dry—no problem, this weather". Taking them off on the grass, I left them and disappeared into the van to make dinner.

A friend had told us beforehand that at the very top of Scotland, and at certain times of the year, it doesn't go properly dark! Our intention was to camp overnight at our newly found site with the clear and beautiful loch on our doorstep. After dinner was finished, washed down with a delicious glass of chilled wine; we both washed the dishes and settled down for the remains of the evening. Dusk was falling now and not having neighbours for miles, we left the blinds and curtains open to look out of the windows of the van. Birds and other wildlife were doing last minute scavenging for food before nightfall. We had seen buzzards circling high above over the mountains, making their familiar mewing noises earlier in the day. But eerie and total hush had fallen now and the scenery began to look like a negative picture with the trees silhouetted against the darkening sky, reflecting down into the dark waters of the loch. The moon had come out and it was casting a reflection into the water and making it sparkle.

"It's dark, but not dark", I said to Chris as we both stared, fascinated out of the window.

"I would love the chance to see the 'Northern Lights' Chris countered, but it's difficult to know exactly when to come up here as you are not always guaranteed to see them depending on clear or cloudy skies".

Returning home, we had made a long list of 'acceptable' and 'non acceptable' things we were looking for inside and outside our new prospective motor home. It took just under 2 years to find our ideal van, by then we had narrowed down the places we wanted to purchase from. As we passed this particular showroom regularly, we got to know the salesman quite well. One day, we happened to see and look around a second hand one which 'ticked all the boxes' for us regarding our requirements. Speaking to the salesman he told us that it had been sold already, but there was another new one at their other depot and that he could arrange for it to be brought there. We eagerly agreed, and waited in anticipation for the salesman to contact us to come and inspect it. That was in the spring of 2006.

It was like furnishing another home again, and for the first few times we took the van away for a weekend break, there was always something we had forgotten to buy or bring with us, like a little knife or some towels. We treated it as a joke in the end by saying that premature dementia had set in, and we were '2 OLD FARTS AND A MOTOR HOME'—So what could we do!!!!

One thing we had both insisted on whilst looking was—you may well guess??

It was a permanent bed!!!

There it was, a thick and comfortable double divan bed—to us, the rest was bonus. It has plenty of room, as it is a 2 berth motor home, for adults only!!! At the end of a good walking day and a hot shower, one of us can crash out full stretch on the bed and read (I usually bag that) and the other can turn the front driver/passenger seats around to make a lounge seat with one, and rest their weary legs and feet on the other seat. We have a roomy fridge/freezer as standard, lots of wardrobe and cupboard space. A very efficient oven and gas hob with one of the hobs being electric so that you can save your gas bottle whilst on a campsite and use it with the electric hook up facility. The shower cubicle is very spacious, we have used it a few times when we have had enough water in the tank to spare, and not had shower facilities on a particular site.

We have learnt a lot of the 'tricks of the trade' so to speak. Such as saving a half dozen large plastic bottles and filling them with fresh drinking water before leaving home or leaving a camp site. We put them in the deep door pockets whilst travelling, only to retrieve them again when we are parked up for the night. Placing them near the kettle on the hob to have a tea or coffee when we are thirsty. We take several different types of connectors with us in our little tool kit whenever we leave home. That is because different sites have different hose connectors at the fresh water terminal. They don't always fit and you end up getting wet feet and trousers trying to hold the end of your hose on to fill the van up. Chris always carries a set of spanners too as well as the mini tool kit; they have proved invaluable over the years for tackling little jobs when we are away from home. This helps with erecting the 'green room' which is a separate room connected to the van by way of upright poles, plastic sides and front with a door. Zipped on along the top to the existing wind out roof awning.

The first time we got on a caravan site and wished to use the green room, it took us three and a half hours!! We laid it all out flat on the grass, and tried to put the poles in the correct place for threading through once we had everything sorted out. I am afraid it didn't work quite as efficiently as we thought it might, and we ended up putting both the sides and the poles the wrong way round and had to start again. We didn't notice at that time, so absorbed in trying to erect the room, but an elderly gentleman who must have been caravanning since Adam was a Lad, had a ring side seat and when we had finally finished he called over to us and said

"It took me 6 hours the first time I did that, you have both done really well; it was less than half of my time".

I must say it broke the tension which had built up out of sheer frustration, and we ended up laughing about it. As before that, we could have quite easily put the whole lot in the communal bins further down the site. Now it takes us a respectable 15/20 minutes to do it when we work together and a bit longer if Chris does it by himself.

Usually I help him put it up and whilst I am doing other jobs when we are packing up to leave a site, then he takes it down himself.

We split jobs, just as we did at the shop. Never a list or anything like that, we instinctively know what we are about and get on with things, coming together at the end. That way, jobs are done quickly so we can get on with enjoying ourselves. Team work, you see! But there is one job I have never attempted to do and that is to empty the cassette toilet. Chris does that first thing in the morning whilst I do breakfast, the two don't go together, so it's best if we split those jobs. You do notice that the men and women on these sites seem to do the same jobs constantly, maybe it's one of those unwritten rules, we don't know. Apart from going to the communal washing up area! For reasons I don't know about, it is the men who come with their pots and pans, dishes and cutlery neatly stacked (by the wives?) in a large washing up bowl. Do they say, "Off you go now, and don't be too long gossiping to the other men?

They know you see! We women know that when a group of men get together, they are as bad if not worse than their women!!

I have seen sometimes, when I have gone in with my pots and pans—washed them, wiped round and left and the same 2 or 3 guys are still there putting the world to rights! I guess it keeps them out of the women's way for a couple of hours until she is ready to go out for the day.

We joined a caravanning club just after we bought our motor home; it is a yearly subscription, which entitles you to a glossy coloured magazine each month with lots of tips and information along with a subsidized entitlement on all their caravan sites. We have had a lot of help and information from the lovely couples who run these sites, and we have found them to be excellent value for money. All the sites are beautiful, with hot clean showers and toilet facilities. Little shops which sell things you may have run out of or forgotten like us. Landscaped with plenty of well cared lawns and flower beds, colourful in the summer months, it is a great pleasure to use them.

The people who use the campsites are in general lovely people with a few colourful characters thrown in for good measure. It brings to mind of an old gentleman on one particular site at a long weekend we had a few summers ago. Situated quite near our own van, his caravan was just one berth!! The caravan in question was very tiny as you could imagine rather like a child's play house. The caravan, like the gentleman was in advancing years, but quite clean and well cared for. One would say that it was 'well used' and had 'been around the block a few times'.

Anyway, we were sat eating breakfast one morning and not being a nosy or inquisitive person (my husband would disagree). I sat in such a way that my line of vision was directed in a straight line over my husband's left shoulder, so I could get a clear view towards the little caravan. Well, I could see that the elderly gentleman was preparing his breakfast, sort of inside and outside the van. (Well I said it was tiny). His little table came out presently, with a gnome sized chair to match. Then a crisp white cotton table cloth was elaborately thrown over the table. We were both intrigued by this time as I had been giving my husband a running commentary on the ritual. Chris casually swiveled around to get a better look. A few minutes into the ceremony, out came the gentleman carrying a very smart tray with his breakfast, a silver teapot, milk jug and sugar bowl, along with a pretty bone china cup and saucer! The ritual began! After seating himself comfortably, and with his back to us as an advantage. We sat spellbound as he flicked his cloth serviette open and tucked it into his jumper. Leisurely pouring his tea (China or Indian?) and helping himself to milk and sugar, he began eating his lightly boiled eggs out of matching china egg cups.

"Well," my husband said after a few minutes of us both staring intently at a long forgotten breakfast ritual. "Isn't it nice to see that good manners and table etiquette hasn't died off completely".

"Yes, it certainly is, I replied, very refreshing to see".

We both finished our breakfast and started preparing for a new day and another experience, we hoped.

"I wonder if he uses the communal washing up block", I asked Chris as we were a good half hour into our walk that day.

"I cannot see how he could do anything else, Chris replied, after all, you wouldn't say his caravan was exactly roomy, more bijou".

Pausing for a moment, I said "I bet he is one of those men who likes to stand chatting and putting the world to rights. He probably tells them about his morning breakfast tea ritual, what do you think"?

Chris didn't answer; he just shook his head and widened his eyes at me!!

This was the start of our small but regular weekends away in our new motor home, going away when we could arrange for our busy shop to be organized by the staff we had working for us. Sometimes we wouldn't go so far from home, maybe an hour's drive that is all. Other times we would go for three nights to make it a long weekend on a campsite. When the weather was kind to us, we would find some remote out of the way place and 'wild camp' for a night or two, enjoying the peace and tranquility only doing that would offer.

CHAPTER 2
THE COILED SNAKE IN CORFU

The self catering apartment was clean and very basic, as most were 20 years ago. Our apartment was one of thirty clustered around the main reception and restaurant area, with a large communal swimming pool nearby. Most of the staff could speak a bit of English, but those who couldn't, make up for it in their pleasant and eager to please attitude.

Dumping our bags on the bed, we had a quick look round at our apartment, ending in the small bathroom. Oh no! There isn't a shower curtain and the shower head is lying on the floor I said, the bracket must have broken off the wall.

Well there is nothing to be done tonight, I am not going down to reception to report it, it will have to wait until tomorrow, Chris replied.

Next morning, we woke to an azure blue sky and the bright sunshine lit up our room with the promise of a lovely day. Jumping out of bed, yawning and stretching, I padded to the bathroom only to see the shower head curled on the tiled floor again. It's still broken Chris!

What did you think would happen in the night? He replied laughing, that fairies would come and fix it for us?

After breakfast, we decided to have a word with the manager regarding the broken shower. He seemed puzzled when we related our story to him, but eventually agreed to come and take a look. We all trouped in, single file, towards the bathroom. Pointing towards the shower head, we told him that the bracket was missing off the wall and there wasn't a shower curtain. Turning to us, he said, buts its all there, nothing is missing. It's a wet room! He started waving it above his head in a vigorous fashion saying, do this, do this!!

I understand I said, still puzzled but willing to go along with it.

Not broken, not missing, Chris clarified,

No, no! he returned, and gave us a dazzling smile before disappearing out the door and down the stairs again.

Coming back to our apartment, late afternoon from a day trip in our hire car. The sun was still shining, giving an overall brightness and warmth. It made the water in the pool glisten and shine like tiny diamonds on the surface.

Chris called from the kitchen, would you like a sun downer on the terrace before getting showered for dinner?

That would be lovely, very civilized, I replied, laughing.

We sat outside a few minutes later to watch the fiery red sun slowly sink down on the horizon, its rays reflecting against the blue-grey skies with large streaks of jewel colours.

Doesn't the sky look beautiful I said dreamily, taking a sip of my favourite tipple and turning to Chris?

He was staring out towards the sky too and replied, could anything be better than where we are right now Patti? We have had a lovely day.

I'll go first, I said, sliding the patio doors open and stepping into the room. Grabbing a towel off the bed, I stood looking at the shower area with the absence of a curtain and the shower head curled up like a coiled snake waiting to pounce.

Holding the shower head poised, I reached forward to turn the dial to 'on'. Immediately, the powerful jets of water came gushing out, as I had not paid attention to which way the shower head was pointing, consequently it shot out of my hand and then began to do a very efficient job of violently spraying water all over the bathroom.

Oh! No! CHRIS—HELP!! I shouted, until Chris opened the door and said, WHAT are you doing??

ERmmm . . . . it's alright now, I said holding the offending implement down with one foot. I've got it under control.

Glancing round the bathroom all I saw were, wet clothes, a towel and sodden toilet rolls. Everywhere was covered in water, dripping down from the vanity unit over the sink and covering the entire surface of the bathroom floor. Although I had noticed the small grid earlier that day and wondered what it was for, as some of the shower water seemed to be slowly seeping away.

As I raised my head up and looked over to Chris, he was stood motionless, staring back at me and shaking his head.

Well, you see, I said, starting to shake, the cold water drying on me. I turned it to 'on' and it shot out of my hand, like a garden hose does sometimes. Before I could 'catch' it, it made all this mess, wasn't my fault!

The offending 'snake' was now laid quietly slumbering on the tiled floor again. Its not a live snake Patti, and started laughing at me shivering violently. You are supposed to be in control, not the other way round!

He reached for a towel for me to get dry, and muttering in a low voice, barely audible said, now we know why they call it a 'wet room'.

CHAPTER 3
EASTER IN AGIOS NICHOLIAS, CRETE

The very first time we went to the Greek islands was over 20 years ago. It happened to be the beautiful island of Crete. Sophia, a regular customer in our shop, who was born in Athens, met and married a Spanish guy and eventually settled down in Blackpool to raise a family.

One day, we mentioned to her about trying Greece for a week's holiday. She told us enthusiastically; that we should try to go Easter week as there would be huge celebrations on, being the most important date in the Greek calendar. Because it is a moveable feast (it doesn't fall on the same date every year) she would find out what date Good Friday falls on, as that would be day one of the festival.

As good as her word, she returned next day and gave us the dates Easter week fell on for that year, emphasizing it would be well worthwhile going to Crete as it was an exceptionally beautiful island.

At that time, there were a lot more travel agents on the high street than there are now. So one afternoon, we finished work early and called in to a travel agent in Blackpool to book our holiday. We asked the young lady if she had any vacant weeks to coincide with the Easter festive and quoted the dates Sophia had given us.

Ah! Yes, it's the Greek Easter she said and told us briefly what we would see, as she had already been a couple of years previously.

We have some flights to Heraklion with a few half-board left at Agios Nicholias, if you are interested. I think this particular hotel is near the centre of Aggie Nick, around the lagoon.

We asked her for more details regarding what kind of place it was. She said, it was a pretty fishing village, with lots of gaily coloured boats tied up in the semi circular lagoon. A variety of themed restaurants line the stone walkways, serving freshly caught fish to customers on a daily basis by the local fishermen.

That sounds really nice, I said. We were both really keen on her description and Chris asked her to go ahead and secure our booking for those given dates.

Two weeks later saw us packed, driven to the airport and boarding a four and a half hour flight to Heraklion airport, to partake in the traditional Easter week celebrations in Crete.

Our hotel was clean and comfortable with fluffy white towels laid neatly on the bed which was already turned down, revealing crisp linen sheets. Comfortably settled late afternoon, we decided to have a stroll along the side of the lagoon and look at restaurants for our evening meal later that evening. We were lucky enough to be centrally situated at the hotel, and near enough to all the amenities just a few minutes' walk away.

The attractive lagoon side restaurants mostly have an open decking area with pretty cloth covered tables displaying posies of flowers and lit candles. On the roof trellis above a canopy of grapevines cascade down, hung with large bunches of juicy black grapes. Perfumed jasmine flowers, their heavily scented aroma fills the air, blown gently by warm soft winds. Exotic palms and

Mediterranean plants fridge the restaurants giving a lush tropical appearance.

Early evening came and with it the lights were being switched on around the lagoon and in the pretty restaurants, giving a fairy grotto feel as they began to serve food and drink. Looking up at the deep blue velvet sky, with a myriad of stars shining down, we strolled arm in arm in the balmy evening, to take the evening air before eating later.

I've never seen so many stars as this before, I remarked, it's very romantic.

Smiling back at me, Chris said, are you pleased we came Patti, it's a lovely place isn't it? We will have a good holiday this week.

We eventually chose a beautiful restaurant which looked out across the lagoon and towards the harbour lights. This is lovely, I said as we walked up the steps and onto the open decked area. The waiter chose a quiet table for us in the corner, with a very ornate stone fountain nearby, showing many different colours in the water, controlled by concealed lighting.

Lingering over our meal and enjoying a lovely chilled wine, we settled back in light conversation and listened to the cicada's making their familiar chirping noise hidden from view in the shrubs and greenery. It was getting late, as we started to notice several Greek families sitting down at the tables to eat.

They are coming out late for a meal I said to Chris in a low voice, if I ate this time of night, I wouldn't be able to sleep.

Unbeknown to us at that time, we heard later that it is quite the normal way of life for the Greek people to eat late in the evenings. In the summer months when the weather is very hot, they usually finish their work around lunchtime when the sun is at its zenith, resting for a few hours in their homes. Between 5 p.m. and 6 p.m. they will have a small sweet cake usually made with honey and almonds, and a strong black coffee before preparations are made to have their main meal of the day when the evening is cooler. We have noticed since that they will remain seated, eating, drinking or just talking until the wee small hours. Dining is a very social event with the Greek people and very much a part of who they are.

Earlier, we had noticed the large bonfire on a raft in the middle of the lagoon, with some kind of cloth effigy on the top. What would that be for I wonder, pointing over to the lagoon? It isn't bonfire night here as well, they wouldn't be celebrating that. (Bonfire night or Guy Faulkes night is an English festival on the 5th November. Guy Faulkes tried to blow up the Houses of Parliament with gun powder, but was caught before he succeeded. Every year, families have a bonfire or pyre made largely of wood and other combustible materials. Children help to make the 'guy' to burn on the night, accompanied by fireworks. Bonfire toffee and parkin cake are made by the Mothers using dark treacle and the Fathers put large potatoes wrapped in foil around the outer edge of the fire).

Still puzzling over the pyre in the lagoon next morning we decided to ask the receptionist at the hotel. She said it was an effigy of Judas, and the pyre would be lit on Saturday night when the celebrations start with a large firework display. But first, as today is Good Friday, this evening starts with a traditional ceremony, taking place at all the little local churches, where they will carry Christ's funeral bier marking the decent from his cross. The bier will be lavishly decorated by all the women of the parish. After the mass, the men will solemnly carry the bier through the streets from the church, followed by a slow procession of local parishioners.

At the municipal buildings in the town square this afternoon, they will be giving away tall candles and boiled eggs coloured in red cochineal for all the tourists. The shops have beautiful displays in their windows with Easter breads, pretty coloured cakes and sweets.

After breakfast we thought we would go down to the town and take a look for ourselves. True to his word, the shops were really beautifully decorated with plaited breads, easter chicks, chocolate eggs, bows and ribbons. The municipal buildings had some local people outside the door giving the candles and eggs away, confirming that they were to be lit at the appropriate time. We decided to arrange the rest of our day around the forthcoming events later that night, and looked for a suitable place to have a meal mid afternoon. Choosing an attractive taverna in the town, we were warmly welcomed and seated. Our menu came promptly, and after ordering some refreshments, the waitress left us for a few minutes to decide what we would like to eat.

What are 'wives leaves' Chris asked me looking puzzled? Unfamiliar with traditional Greek food in those days, I said, I don't know, but it sounds interesting, why not ask her when she comes back.

She came back after a while with a pad and pencil poised in her hand. 'Er! What are 'wives leaves' my husband asked? Looking over his shoulder to see where he was pointing, she replied. 'AHhhh—that's a typing error, it should read Vine Leaves!!

Smiling up at her Chris said, well we will try those first, they sound interesting. I thought you had taken to cooking and eating women over here! We both started laughing and she saw the funny side of it and laughed too.

Returning later, she not only brought our newly christened 'wives leaves' out but with them a lovely variety of local Greek mezethes, filling the table with a host of delicious food. We asked for some local village wine to accompany the food. She brought us a light fruity white wine which totally complimented the meal.

As darkness fell in the early evening, families and friends came out from their homes to join others to walk towards their own local church. We walked through a maze of narrow streets; we stopped to watch the start of the ceremony from across the road. A group of men were just coming out of the church interior carefully negotiating the ornate bier with lots of colourful flowers and ribbons, a centrally placed cross and four small ornamented domed churches one in each corner. Each bier slightly different from the other churches in the town. Many other local people had gathered round to wait patiently outside and then to walk behind the bier, carried high upon the men's shoulders, behind a slowly growing procession.

On Saturday morning, there was a lovely feeling of excitement and anticipation in the air, as complete strangers walked by us and said hello. Many local people were busily shopping, in preparation for the evening's event. The town started filling up with visitors in the afternoon, who were arriving by car or coach to watch the festival unfold. Fortunately for us, we were already well organized regarding seating arrangements at the restaurant we had used the previous evening, so we could take our table at an agreed time.

When asking the receptionist again that morning, about the next stage of the ceremony.

She said the next lot of events wouldn't happen until just before midnight. The local priest holds mass in the church first to celebrate Christ's return. At the stroke of midnight, all the lights in the crowded church are switched off and the congregation will be plunged into total darkness. This is emulating Christ passing through the underworld. Then behind an alter screen the priest appears, holding a lighted candle saying "This is The Light of the World". Moving down towards his congregation, he lights the unlit candle of the parishioner nearest to himself. They then, turn to their neighbour and light their candle, saying "Come, take the Light".

The time was nearing midnight, the atmosphere was electrifying! In anticipation of the religious events unfolding at the little white washed church suspended, overlooking the lagoon. We could see everything from our table, and we both agreed that we were quite content to let it happen all around us, and absorb the party atmosphere later. We had brought our candles with us, which were laid on the table tied with pretty coloured ribbons at the base.

It's a bit like New Years Eve, I said, looking round at some anxious people checking their watches. Just then, all the lights went out around the lagoon, the bars and restaurants were plunged into darkness, no glimmer of light could be seen. Total hush descended, as people waited, in anticipation.

We heard some movement from the little church above, as everyone held their breath! After a few minutes, the priest must have come out of the church, as we could see one small candle light. We heard his voice saying something, and then soon afterwards, another small light could be seen, shortly followed by another and then another! The candle light cascaded slowly down the steep incline from the church and then round the lagoon, ever nearer to us until we both stood up and our neighbours on the next table said "Come, take the Light". She held her candle out to light mine first and then Chris'. We all shook hands and hugged each other; I felt totally overwhelmed and started crying. We joined in to wish everyone nearby a very Happy Easter. (We were told by the receptionist, the local people will carefully carry their lit candles home again, and if they reach their door and the candle is still alight, they believe it will bring good fortune to their home).

Let the celebrations begin we said laughing with delight as, seated once more, and in full view of the newly lit pyre; we could see the flames shooting high into the night sky. Loud crackling and spitting emitted as we briefly saw a burning Judas disappearing into the flames.

As Chris ordered a chilled bottle of wine from the waiter to toast Easter Day. Fireworks exploded around us in a myriad of colours—high into the velvety dark blue skies. 'Her own' display already formed in the contrasting brightness of many twinkling stars in the solar system.

Next day—Easter Sunday, after a leisurely breakfast and nursing an aching head! We made arrangements to have a drive into the mountains and see how the mountain folk celebrate their Easter Sunday. We saw a whole community in one village, come together and share a huge feast in the tiny square. Families visited parents who were roasting a whole lamb on a spit in the garden. Others were seated, 20 or more family members around a very large table, laughing and talking whilst they ate, with younger family members playing nearby. It's not unusual to see 5 generations in one family. The village wine flowed and the raki was sat waiting for the brave and foolish to drink later.

The Greek people love to celebrate with friends and family. Their beautiful country is steeped in traditions and history, which they embrace with reverence and enthusiasm.

From this first holiday experience we both shared our growing affection towards Greece and the Greek people. It was the very beginning of many enjoyable experiences to come over the following years.

CHAPTER 4
BUYING THE VILLA AT AGIA TRIADA

It all started one Sunday morning in February 2007 when Chris went to our village shop to buy a newspaper. After breakfast, and finishing his coffee, he commented on an interesting advertising article in the paper offering a subsidized 3 day holiday for potential purchasers, to view various residential building developments in Crete.

This will give us the added advantage of being shown different areas, with a knowledgeable guide, Chris remarked. They are having an open day in Bolton Lancashire next weekend; shall we go and see what it is all about?

The following Sunday, we drove down to Bolton, and found the open day at the local football ground. Parking our car, we entered the single storey building belonging to the club, to be greeted by a smiling young lady, smartly dressed and sitting behind a desk in the large room. On the walls were beautiful pictures of Crete, some newly built properties, and an artist impression of the building project? We spent a few minutes looking at them before being invited to sit down by a middle aged gentleman.

Introductions were made, and then he proceeded to tell us all about the company, who represented several builders on their behalf.

It gives the prospective buyer a chance to view a much wider range of properties which have already been built and others in the process of being built.

We were talking to him for over 2 hours, many questions asked, and answered in a measured and professional manner. He moved away from his desk to let us talk amongst ourselves, so as not to feel pressurized. We decided to make an appointment to take up the offer of a three day visit to Crete. At a mutually consented date, the company would fly us out to Heraklion where we would be met by a representative at the airport. Arrangements had already been made for us to stay in an hotel conveniently situated in the centre of Rethymnon.

An early morning flight of four and half hours saw us land smoothly at the airport and collecting our luggage, we were met by a pleasant English guy holding a cardboard sign up with our names on it. Grinning, he introduced himself as Darren and said that his car was parked outside to take us to our hotel. Helping us with the luggage, we were comfortably settled in the car and speeding along towards Rethymnon town. As he drove, he started telling us that he came to Crete 2 years ago with his wife and 2 children. They were all happy and settled and were renting a villa in one of the villages.

As he dropped us off at the hotel, he said that he would come back later to take us for an evening meal. Returning at 7-00 p.m. in reception, we were rested and refreshed and looking forward to our evening meal. Over dinner at a delightful restaurant in Rethymnon town, we relaxed and got to know each other quite well. It was 11-00 p.m. and Chris and I both felt tired after a long day. Excusing ourselves to Darren, he then kindly took us back to our hotel for the night, with a pre-arranged appointment to come back after breakfast and start the guided tour.

Showing us several properties around Rethymnon prefecture, he asked us a few questions regarding our thoughts, and the type of property we were interested in.

After a little while, he said, Ah! I think I have something which maybe just what you are looking for. Turning the wheel of his car, he headed towards the village of Platanas.

The village of Platanas hums constantly through the busy holiday season, with lovely shops, hotels and restaurants. In the winter months, it still has a lot to offer with the local Greek people regularly meeting up for a coffee and a chat. Or using the restaurants and night club situated in the square.

Turning right, past the fleet of stationary taxi's parked and waiting on the rank, we drove up the road passing a few large and well kept houses surrounded by olive groves. We were beginning to like the feel of this area, as it would not become a 'ghost town' when the summer visitors had gone home. We had in mind that we would love to come and spend a few months at a time, summer and winter once we had retired from work.

A short while later, Darren signalled the car, and drove up a steep incline, passing a few more well tended olive groves on each side of the road. Eventually, we get our first views of the partially ruined village of Agia Triada perched high on a hill, overlooking a great expanse of olive groves and across to the mountains beyond.

We had driven to the head of the ravine, and as the road became narrower—it wound its way steeply up and past an old water well which would have once served the village. Now unused and unloved, it gives shelter to an old and battered pickup truck.

The young man swung his car expertly past a traditional farm, and down a very bumpy dirt track road to come to an abrupt stop. I whispered to Chris in the backseat, 'where is he taking us' I feel like we've been kidnapped'. With a re-assuring smile, he got out of the car and held the door open for me to do the same.

Come and look at this. He walked towards an elevated piece of land with a few olive trees and some poor quality grazing for goats. "The builder who owns this land is going to build four properties here, with a centrally placed swimming pool and then landscaped.

There were beautiful views of the olive groves over the low stone wall, and up to the mountains beyond. The head of the gorge has a vast amount of greenery, shrubs and wild herbs, running along and out towards the sea.

It's really nice here I said presently, very peaceful, and so quiet you can hardly hear anything at all, only occasional farm noises. We both stood quite still for a while, absorbing all around us and looked up to follow the noise of three buzzards flying and circling above us, riding the thermals and calling in their familiar 'mewling' cry.

Safely returned to the hotel once more, we made an appointment with Darren to see the builder in question next day. He would also arrange to have a solicitor appointed to us at the same time. Leaving us and deep in thought by our exciting but also daunting next step, we spoke about nothing else for the rest of the day. We had heard of so many stories. People like us coming to buy property abroad and it all ending in tears!

Exhausted, we fell into bed later that night after further discussions with Darren who assured us that this particular builder was an honourable man. He is an established architect and builder, and would be doing both jobs, he told us. Darren knew that he had built other properties in Rethymnon town, and had heard nothing but excellent reports on the quality of his work.

Deciding next morning to keep an open mind and listen to what the builder had to say regarding costs, legalities and when the building project was likely to be finished.

A short journey with Darren to Rethymnon centre, we were following him through the builder offices for our morning appointment. Formal greetings and introductions were made and then we all sat round the builder desk.

It was the first time we had met our appointed lady solicitor that day, and over the years following, she has become a very capable and trusted friend. We feel that if we need to know anything, or have any worries at all concerning the complex Greek law, she has told us to call her, and she will do her best to sort it out.

From that day, the wheels were set in motion, as step by step, we were taken through each stage of the plans, designs, legal and financial aspects. Every stage was explained in great detail and with unending patience. When the initial building had begun, we decided to have a few modifications in our villa. These included a larger bathroom so we could have a Jacuzzi bath, as well as a shower. We have found that most Greek properties have small bathrooms, and have their washing machines in there too. We enjoy our Jacuzzi bath at home in England, and thought we could have the affordable luxury of cool bubbles in the hot summer when we get overheated, or a nice hot bubbly bath in the winter when we come back from walking in the mountains. A chilled glass of village wine and a good book, what more could you want??

Returning to England after our mind blowing three days, our heads full of building plans, schedules and legalities etc. We need not to have been concerned as together, our lovely solicitor and a patient and understanding builder kept us constantly informed with everything we needed to know.

Through constant pressure of work, coupled with my husband's visit to hospital and a long recuperation, we could not go out to see the start of the building project. Very thoughtfully, some close friends, Sue and Richard, booked a week's holiday and purposefully went over to see how things were progressing and take lots of pictures for us. Closely followed by some more friends who did the same. It was exciting, but also re-assuring, that the construction was going well and the building was on a constant daily basis, to be finished around their initial target date.

As we were the first ones to pay our deposit, we could choose which plot we wanted. We chose the single storey villa at the furthest end of the complex. There, we would have the lovely views of the olive groves and the magnificent views of the mountains and gorge leading down to the sea. The pool would be painted in Mediterranean blue, surrounded by a landscaped garden, suitably planted with a contrasting assortment of brightly coloured flowers. Framed by tall palms and oleander trees which flower all summer long, and give maximum shelter and privacy. A single, outdoor shower, warmed by the summer sun would be placed near the pool, and nearby the boiler room with all the relevant dials and switches.

Eventually, Chris was well enough again to book us on a flight from Manchester and go out to see our new villa, as it was now nearing completion. The builder's secretary informed us by e mail, that we could get the keys from her at the office to look round and then let them know if they needed to alter or adjust any building work to suit our needs. We booked some conveniently situated apartments not far from Rethymnon, so we would be near the shops and restaurants, and to attend appointments with the solicitor and builder.

Our hire car this time was a small 4 wheel drive, with a soft top, because the early spring weather brought the warm sunshine. Driving along the mountain roads the sweet scents from the wild herbs fill your nostrils.

An early morning flight again, and we were walking over towards the car hire office just around lunchtime. Paperwork done and signed for, she told us that it was the white vehicle in the parking lot, and then asked where we were going.

Chris replied, a place called Gerani, but we are not sure how to get there.

Giving directions, she added, at the moment, they are doing extensive road works and you have to make an illegal left hand turn, but don't worry, everybody does it here, it's the only way to get across.

We were quite stunned, but said nothing, only a thank you for her helpful directions. It's strange, because as I write this, it doesn't seem so shocking now, just quite normal over here.

Piling our cases into the car, Chris opened the top and folded it back as it was such a lovely day and we would enjoy the warm breeze as we travelled along the National Road. I watched for road signs, as Chris familiarized himself with how the traffic was progressing and where everything was in the car. As long as we straddled the nearside white line and kept well in when not overtaking, the locals will quite happily zoom past at an amazing speed. But let concentration go for a moment—and oh boy!! They drive right up to the tailgate, flashing their lights and sounding their horn. An uneventful journey, we quickly found our accommodation and settled in for the day.

Can you remember where the builder offices are in Rethymnon? I said, next morning. We had decided to buy some breakfast in the town and do some food shopping for breakfast and snacks midday.

I have a good idea Chris replied, we haven't got our appointment from Susan the secretary yet, so it might be a good idea to try and find it today.

We used the car park in the centre of Rethymnon and set off walking in the general direction of what we could vaguely remember last time we were there. Walking down the high street, nothing seemed familiar, so we then cut down another road which ran parallel to the high street. Still nothing! Now what? I said beginning to panic, should we ask someone?

Not just yet, we can always ask Susan when she phones us to confirm our appointment.

We looked for the big school as a landmark which we remembered was near the office. Eventually, we gave up and decided to go into the Old Town and do some shopping.

The next day our mobile rang, it was Susan to give us the appointment and meet her in the office. Chris said that we had already tried to find her office and failed and she said we were quite near, just one street away in fact.

Keeping our appointment on the day, and over a coffee, we all had a good laugh as we retold our story about getting lost. She offered to show us a local furniture shop nearby, and a short walk brought us to a small local shop over stuffed with everything for the home. As the young Greek lady showed us round, Susan translated to her as to what we wanted, making communication a lot easier. We were both admiring a large settee in the far corner, and Susan told us that it was actually a double bed settee. Oh! This is just what we have in mind for the living area for when friends and family come to stay I said.

After a short conversation with the shop assistant, she translated to us that it would be hand made at the shop and you may choose from a large book of swatches for the fabric covering. Both sitting down on the settee whilst the young lady brought an enormous book bulging with every fabric available, it didn't take long before we eventually selected them. One for the overall covering; and a contrast for the back of the settee and cushions.

We had spotted some beds, single and double ones as we came through the shop door; it took a few minutes to decide what we would like.

As we came out into the bright sunshine again, Susan asked us if we had made prior arrangements regarding electrical goods.

No, not yet, we both said.

So what about me take you down to a big electrical shop further down in the town? They have everything there you will need.

Strolling along in the sunshine, she asked us what our immediate needs were.

A cooker and a fridge/freezer was the reply. Also a kettle and an orange juicer as well.

It was a very busy, modern electrical shop crammed full of absolutely everything you would need, just as Susan promised it would be. I was in seventh heaven looking at all the gadgets, cookers, fridges and puzzling over some items which we do not see in England and was explained away by a shop assistant. We eventually chose a lovely cooker with glass hobs and a large fridge/freezer which will fit very nicely into the space provided back at our villa.

Leaving the shop, we both thanked her once more as she asked if it would be okay to take us to see our villa in a couple of days as she had another appointment with a client soon. We nodded in agreement.

Leaving her to walk back to the office, we decided to familiarize ourselves with the town of Rethymnon.

We have both grown to love Rethymnon because it is a busy working town. The shops sell good quality merchandise and you can probably find almost anything you require here, on the high street or the weekly outdoor market based in the centre.

Wander into the old town, with its fascinating mix of Venetian and Turkish architecture; their ancient wooden balconies and solid wooden doors bleached with years of constant sun and wind. Unusual curiosity shops are tucked away down the narrow passageways, shaded by high sided buildings to keep them cool from the hot summer sun. Time served craftsmen, concentrate on creating their wooden lyras, (the Cretan violin) to make the popular local music, sit inside the open doorways of their musty shops.

Another little shop, with the familiar Turkish arched stone ceiling holds an inordinate amount of dusty old brassware. Hanging lanterns and incense burners decorate the low ceiling. The low windowsill in the shop is packed tightly with every brass ornament you would want, along with some old genie lamps, the kind you would see in the Arabian Knights or Aladdin.

Wander further along, we see yet another unusual shop selling the traditional Cretan costume. The owner, a big guy around seven foot high can be seen walking round the old town or at the many celebratory parades wearing the full National dress, and looking very impressive.

Calling in for refreshments later that day, we walked into the most amazing tavern we have ever seen. It was literally overstuffed with a vast collection of bric-a-brac, pictures, and old farming tools. The silly and the serious, covering all the walls, ceiling, and floor space, jostling with small iron tables and chairs. We spent the first half an hour, just wandering around and looking at this remarkable display which must have taken years to collect.

After a while, the jolly Greek lady who introduced herself as Maria, told us that this building was originally a prison where the Cretan prisoners were held under Turkish occupation. Pointing to a low wooden door at the end of a dark passageway, she invited us to come and take a peep. We followed her into a dank and musty room, bereft of any windows or natural light. An old Turkish brass lantern was suspended from the stone arched ceiling, and the remains of manacles and chains hung from the stone wall in the far corner of the room. We gasped in awe as she told us that this prison was used regularly during Turkish occupation which spanned a 230 year period!

I shuddered, as I felt the pain and sadness emanating from the room. What these poor people must have suffered didn't bear thinking about.

We thanked her warmly for taking the time and trouble to show us something which had long since been filed away in the history archives, but something that should not be entirely forgotten, so we never repeat such atrocities again.

We were drawn towards the magnificent Venetian fortezza at the very top of Rethymnon, its ancient angular building with a distinctive ochre dome rising up over the harbor. It is the largest Venetian castle ever built, to protect the town from constant raids by marauding pirates which, over time, looted the fortezza.

Designed by an Italian engineer, it took 10 years to build at enormous cost, but large enough for the entire population of Rethymnon to seek refuge when under attack. Eventually falling into the hands of the Turkish Empire, there were several other buildings added, including the restyling of the church interior, thus making a mosque dedicated to the ruling sultan Ibrahim. Recently renovated with a beautiful dome and a pretty carved mihrab (a niche indicating the direction of Mecca) it brings a regular flow of visitors up to the huge double gates of the fortezza.

As I write, further restorations are taking place in the centre of Rethymnon near the old town. The first building is a single storey domed mosque near the palm tree lined promenade. With some final restoration still to do, beautifully carved stone pillars lay waiting in the gated area of the mosque, to eventually be situated in their original home. Nearer the old town, stands a large stone obelisk completely surrounded by scaffolding. Comprehensive work is being done to repair and restore the intricately carved obelisk which is attached to an old Turkish mosque.

So much history! So much to see. It's all here waiting for visitors to come and discover the True Spirit of Crete!!!

It was an exciting morning when we met our secretary Susan, to drive us up to look at our new villa. On the way, we asked her how the bed settee was coming along. She told us that the beds and mattress would be delivered whenever you want them, and the settee was almost finished, and will be delivered all together from the shop for when you come over next time.

I will arrange to have it all delivered to the villa when you e mail me you are coming over next time.

That's brilliant! And an enormous help, we are hoping to come out again in a few weeks, and bring with us a lot of other things we have bought in England.

Arriving at the double gates and the entrance to the complex, we jumped out of her four wheel drive and walked through. We had already seen several photos of the pool and garden, but it was so much better and more exciting to be standing surrounded by it all.

It's hard to believe that the last time we were here; it was just a field with a few olive trees I said. The garden surrounding the pool was still in the process of being landscaped, the black membrane was down over the soil to help stop the weeds. Some of the young trees and shrubs were already planted, giving the overall effect of how the garden would look in a few years time.

'Now here is YOUR new home' Susan said with a smile, as she put the key in the door. Taking a deep breath, we walked in, single file to look round at our beautiful villa. The light coloured tiles on the floor were really clean and light, and the kitchen units in a light oak, gave an overall effect of brightness for the summer months. 'You have a large fireplace and full central heating should you wish to be here in the winter months, she added.

'Come and look at the bathroom Patti, Chris said, it has our Jacuzzi fitted. Walking into the main bedroom we opened the patio door to admire the views of the mountains and the lush greenness of the gorge below.

Well, what do you think of your finished home, Susan asked. We told her we were both very happy with the building work and the finished quality of the villa and thanking her profusely, she promised to tell her boss our reaction.

A few days later, we returned home to England and did quite a bit more shopping to take with us to Crete. Previously pricing bedding in Rethymnon, we decided to buy it all in England and bring them out with us, vacuum sealed in a suitcase. We had already, a growing pile of 'useful items' which we had bought and stored away upstairs to bring with us. Now, the pile had grown into a small hill, as we started to pack it all into our overly large suitcase. We agreed that the suitcase was a tad on the heavy side, but shouldn't prove a hindrance

Little did we realize then, but on our return visit, arriving at the airport early one morning, we joined the queue of travelers until it was our turn to 'check in'. The young lady asked us the mandatory questions before asking Chris to put the luggage onto the conveyor belt.

Is it just one suitcase, she asked, looking at the screen.

Yes, it is and we have got some hand luggage too, Chris replied.

You are over the weight limit, she said, looking at Chris accusingly.

I didn't know what to say, but Chris told me afterwards, that my mouth opened and shut like a goldfish, with nothing coming out! (Unusual for me, he commented afterwards).

Ah! Chris said, regaining his composure, by how much?

She proceeded to tell him the kilo weight, and said it will cost you sixty pounds if you want to take it all. Pay at the desk over there she said pointing, then turned her attention to the couple behind us.

Chris dragged the heavy suitcase off the conveyor belt, and we shuffled away, both of us feeling like naughty children who had got found out. Still speechless, I trudged behind him to the desk in question, where, producing a docket the young lady had given us, reluctantly parted with sixty pounds of our hard earned holiday money. Eventually, my voice started working again, and I said in a low voice, we might as well have bought our stuff in Rethymnon town, as we joined the queue once again to 'check in'.

Chris turned to me and with a smile, lesson learnt Patti, lesson learnt!!

We had booked a hire car to be collected at Heraklion airport on arrival. We had previously instructed Susan to have the furniture delivered to our villa ahead of schedule. It was early evening by the time we touched down and collected 'that suitcase' from off the carousel, and dragged it out through the airport and the small car hire offices.

It was the first time we had driven from the airport at night, and we were comparative strangers to the layout of the roads leading away from the airport, unsure of how the roads joined the National Road; and not confident of when to leave the National Road to find our villa in the foothills. And it was DARK!!

I'm a bit scared, I said to Chris, as I watched him heave the suitcase into the back seat of the car, being too large to fit in the back storage boot.

Don't worry, came his usual reply, we will be okay!

I love him for that, always looks at the cup of life being half full—

Me, usually it's half empty and then I start worrying again.

The start of our journey was relatively straight forward, as there was only one way out of the airport, and large, clearly marked signs told us we were on our way to Rethymnon.

Ah! That was easy I said, relaxing into my car seat and eying up the big ugly red suitcase bobbing about at the back.

Everything looked so different and much darker as we drove along the quiet road, grateful for very few vehicles, which sped past us as we safely straddled the white line and kept out of their way.

Presently, Chris announced that he thought we were about half way there to the turn off at Platanas.

I told him I had brought the details with me on how to find our villa in the dark, posted to us from Doreen and Clive when they visited our villa last year to take a look at the building work in progress.

We came to a halt under the bridge at Platanas to check on the instructions. Soon, we were off again, and climbing up the winding road leading to our new home. Slowing down, hesitantly, as the street lighting became infrequent, and then disappeared altogether. All we had was the beam from the headlights of our car. Several feral cats ran across our path out of the trash bins, alerted by the noise of our car engine. A beautiful barn owl flew out from one of the deserted crumbling ruins of the old Agia Triada, intent on catching its prey.

We had finally arrived, it was very late by then and we were really tired after such a long journey. Turning the key, Chris had been already told by Susan that the builder had kindly 'temporarily wired up' an electricity cable from his supply so we could be comfortable whilst there until we were connected properly by the local Electricity Company in Crete. There was also a complimentary bottle of wine and chocolates waiting for us as a welcoming gift from the builders.

All our furniture had been delivered and whilst Chris wrestled with the heavy suitcase, I waited to unpack the bedding.

We both slept deep and long and woke to bright warm sunshine. We have said many times since; we have THE best view from our bathroom window into the olive grove and the back drop of slate grey mountains beyond.

Hurrying down to the local supermarket in Platanas, I remarked we didn't need a shopping list, when we have nothing at all in the cupboards, and laughed. At this time, the euro was worth 1.46 to us, and made shopping a joy.

It took us well over an hour to get everything we needed including cleaning materials, as by now, the villa had a small collection of assorted bugs, most of them never seen before by us. Now I am not squeamish, but I think I have done more squealing, yelping and ugh-ing than I have ever done!

Let's see—they have a black worm like creature, which has the capacity to wriggle under the front door and end up in some strange places. A friend of mine, nicknamed them 'curly whirlies' when she actually found one in her bed one night! I won't repeat what she said when she found it, but needless to say, she pulls the duvet right back every night and inspects the bed before getting in. We have seen quite a few very large spiders; we have heard they eat other insects in the houses. There is a scarab like beetle too, impressive to look at outdoors, but very daunting when viewed inside the villa.

One afternoon recently after moping the floors of the villa I went to sit outside in the sunshine. Engrossed in my novel, I felt something quite hard bang against my arm. Looking down, there was the biggest bug I have ever seen laid on its back motionless, with its legs in the air. It must be dead, I thought, and continued reading. A minute or so passed, and I glanced down at it again, only to see to my dismay, that it had righted itself again. It must have knocked itself out banging against my arm, I thought. Fascinated, I leaned over to get a closer look, it was staring back at me with what looked like protruding white eyes. It had a hard dark shell of a body with its wings folded back against the sides, with grass hopper style legs.

Oh!! Ugh!! I said, getting up quickly, and what kind of creature are you then?

Grabbing my chair and book, I retreated to the other side of the patio in an attempt to put some distance between us.

Of course, we have the pretty little gecko's here, I love them, even though they move very quickly. Being such timid shy creatures, we know they wouldn't harm you and locals welcome them into their homes to eat mosquitoes and other small bugs.

Last, but by no means least, the dreaded mosquito. You would not think such a small creature could do so much damage to the people skin at certain times of the year. Hearing their high pitched drone sends me scurrying away to get some mozzie spray and zap them. We both have a terrible reaction to their bite, the results looking like we have ulcerated legs, with open weeping blisters. Consequently, we have a bathroom cabinet stuffed full of various lotions and potions to relieve and cure.

Returning to the villa, with a vast amount of shopping, it was time to eat. We didn't have a table and chairs then, but it didn't matter, we had a lovely picnic sat on the lower steps by the pool in the sunshine. This holiday is very memorable to us, the start of a new life, the pleasure we got from 'making do' even going without a full complement of furniture. It turned into a big joke, as half way through making a meal, I would require something like a colander to drain the vegetables—no colander!!

It helped a lot when we drove our motor home over from England stuffed to bursting with all sorts of household requirements. We really did load that vehicle down with a huge amount of items, large and small. A large fireguard from Jackie, my sister in law, two reclining sun chairs, which were a lot cheaper in England than Crete. Quite a few work tools belonging to Chris, for him to do D.I.Y jobs in the villa. Erecting curtain rails, and putting light fittings up etc.

By the time we had packed everything we thought we would need in the motor home, I asked Chris if there was any room left for us, ha ha . . . The cupboards and the boot were packed to bursting with a large assortment of goods. The fridge was full to capacity, and the storage space under the bench was full with tinned stuff and dry goods. Climbing up the steps into the van, I watched Chris loading our double bed with pillows, the duvet and sheets etc. Well, where are we sleeping then? I asked innocently.

Frowning for a moment, in deep thought, he eventually said. Well if we put that there, and then bring this over here, we can sleep there, and in the morning . . . .

Ah! I get the picture, I said nodding slowly, and we are going to play a game of drafts.

Then we both burst out laughing!!!!

CHAPTER 5
ENGLAND TO CRETE

1st SEPTEMBER 2010 to 15th FEBRUARY 2011

Once we decided to 'go for it', that is, drive our motor home from North West England to our villa in Crete, Greece; we were full of enthusiasm and very excited.

The adventure wasn't a snap decision, it took us almost 2 years of organizing, planning and with many arrangements to be made.

Looking at our map book of Europe in the evenings and making never ending lists of what to do, and how to do it. The detailed planning was good and gave us both something to focus on and look forward to the future. Chris had been poorly and this made us both feel very positive to be able to plan our lives.

We realized almost right away that it was impossible to just disappear, as the house would be empty for 6 months. We decided to let someone we knew, live there and keep it warm and occupied. The utility companies had to be contacted, bills paid up front, cancelling regular delivery and our mail re-directed to my sister-in-law's house. We needed to put our furniture into storage.

My Mother always said 'you should move every 7 years'. So whilst you pack your things away in boxes, you can throw out all the stuff you do not need or use. She was right, methodically sifting through my drawers and cupboards one day, determined that I will not pack things we do not need in the future. I remarked to Chris when he walked into the bedroom and looked at a growing pile of things on the bed.

I think we'll do a car boot sale, I said, you know I hate clutter. Its an ideal opportunity to do it now before we put everything into storage.

Turning to me, he nodded sagely and replied, It's a good thing I am still useful, or you'd be selling me off as well.

Pausing for a moment, to think of a witty answer, I said, Do you know my love, I would, but you are too big to display on top of the decorating table.

Catching his eye, we both burst into peals of laughter.

Anyone who has ever done a car boot will relate to my next paragraph with knowledgeable humour. For uninitiated, this is how it happened:

We organized a date one Sunday between ourselves and with my sister and brother in law, eventually deciding to do a car boot sale near their home. They also had some things to sell, and with their grandson, Ryan growing fast; a lot of his toys and baby clothes would be found a useful home.

We drove from Jackie's house at 4-00 a.m. full of expectations. It was coming day break as we found the field in question. Many cars had already formed a long queue to find the best pitch, and have the added advantage of being seen by customers first.

We had loaded our estate car the night before, packing it right up to the top of the roof inside with all our things. As always, in England, even on a summer morning, there is always a sharp nip in the air until the sun peeps through to warm us up. So it was that morning, we had got our thick jumpers and trousers on, coupled with boots and rain proofs incase the weather turned cold and wet. A few others had come onto the field already, and were setting their stalls out.

Do you think we should have come here earlier, I said to Chris looking round at the other organized stall holders.

No, definitely not, he replied, laughing, this is early enough for me these days.

Pulling onto a suitable pitch, we opened the back boot of the car to unfold the decorating table. Without warning, two or three people walked towards the boot and without ceremony, started rummaging around in the back of the car.

Where did THEY come from? Jackie whispered to me, as I stood in amazement watching them.

What the heck is going on, exclaimed Chris, looking at an untidy pile of clothes thrown around the car.

How much do you want for this, a burly looking man enquired, in a deep voice?

Er! I don't know yet, I squeaked back, feeling like a compete novice.

By then, discarded newspaper wrapping was spilling out onto the grass, as the other two opportunists broke into an excited frenzy as to who could reach the bottom of the boxes first to find an antique treasure or a valuable painting.

Taking the lead, the burly guy said, I'll give you two pounds, take it or leave it. By now, the four of us were rendered speechless as we continued to watch, fascinated, as the others continued to throw our stuff round the car. Eventually, I found my voice, and with my confidence fast draining away, I slowly nodded a yes!

He put the two pounds in my hand and strode away. We still had the other 3 rebels to contend with. Just then, Jackie caught my eye, and in a low voice she said, "if we don't stop them soon, we will all be buried in a sea of newspaper"

Ahem!—Er—excuse me, could you please stop that now, I er, think you've seen most of it, I said.

How much for this lady, one of the trio asked, it's got a chip on it, so it will not be worth much. I'll give you a pound.

No, can you leave NOW, Chris shot back, all brave and masterful!

Turning in unison, they wandered back down the field again.

Well, Bill said, they were something else eh? We'd better get cracking now or the car boot will be over before we have managed to set up. We didn't take too long between us and perching on the back of the open boot, we had our breakfast and waited for our first customers.

An elderly guy walked over to us grinning, I see you've met the regulars then, he said. Oh! Yes, they WERE a bit pushy, regular customers looking for a bargain, I said.

Throwing back his head, he started laughing. No, they are regular stall holders; they do this for a living. They come here every Sunday, and if they see some new faces, they take advantage because they are on the lookout for a bargain to sell on THEIR STALL!!!

He started laughing again as he walked away shaking his head.

Huh! I said, eating my sandwich, they must think we are a right load of 'idiots'.

Well, we are, Chris muttered quietly!

That wasn't too bad, Jackie remarked as we got back to their house that afternoon. We have sold quite a bit of stuff between us. The best thing is that we have sold some of Ryan's toys, so he won't be looking in the boxes and then re-claiming them. We might have to do another car boot sale before going to Crete I said, but next time we will keep a watch for marauding pirates attacking the car.

The months flew by, and we were starting to count the weeks leading up to our 'trip of a lifetime'. It's getting nearer to our holiday, I said one morning, we will have to start sorting through all our furniture soon, and decide what we want to put into storage, and what we want to sell. As we had a few nice pieces of antique furniture, collected over the years, we thought we would sell a few of them to raise some pocket money.

From our telephone directory, and a few initial enquiries, we settled on a reputable dealer who was locally based. Making an appointment for him to call one afternoon, we told him our address. He told me in his very attractive Italian accent, he did not know this area. So alternative arrangements were made to meet him on the car park of our local village public house. At the appointed time, I was approached by a smartly dressed elderly gentleman, wearing expensive Italian clothes. His white hair neatly cut and swept back from his tanned face. Extending his hand and with a warm friendly smile said 'Ello'. My name is Lawrence. How do you do, I replied, and pointing across the road, told him my house wasn't far away.

His eyes darted round the lounge as I invited him in, and pursing his lips for a moment, asked me what items I would be selling. The transactions went very well, and we were soon loading my beautiful furniture into the back of his transit van. Asking me what our future plans were, I told him that amongst other countries, we would be driving down the North East Coast of Italy. His eyes misted over as he assured me how beautiful Italy was.

I felt a twinge of loss and regret as Lawrence closed the car boot on my furniture, lovingly polished over the years. But common sense prevailed, as he handed over the money for the deal! Remembering how much money was going to be needed over the coming months.

Chris came in later from working, and observing the large empty spaces in the house, said, we are on our way now Patti. We will have a holiday of a lifetime.

Time was marching on and our next priority was to search for a reliable local storage company. Out came the directory! A few enquiries and phone calls and we found just what we needed a few miles away. Pressure started to grow the nearer it got to 1st September. It became so strong at one point; I would wake in the middle of the night, and jump out of bed to add something else to our long list of 'to do'. Try to put things out of your mind before going to bed, Chris remarked one night, you will be worn out before the adventure begins otherwise.

At an appointed time, we drove down to the storage company and being ushered in by the manager, finalized all our details and requirements. We will need packing boxes, bubble wrap and tape I said. He advised us on how to pack the boxes, and other useful tips and bade us goodbye until the removal day came. Our methodical sorting, wrapping and packing the boxes began. Trying to do something every day, there seemed to be a never ending pile of things needing attention.

Our list was slowly growing smaller now as the days dwindled away. The holiday was constantly on our minds, coupled with wondering if we had remembered to do everything. Over breakfast one morning, I mentioned to Chris about re-directing the post. Yes, it was on the list, he said, I have already made arrangement with Jackie and Bill to have it sent to their house.

He added, I am going to look for a suitable ferry crossing today. I think it would be better if we drive to Hull and use their ferry crossing over to Rotterdam.

Three hours later, he emerged, triumphantly saying he found just what we needed, although it will be an overnight sailing leaving at 7-00p.m. and arriving early next morning in the port of Rotterdam.

Nervously, I said, have you booked yet Chris?

Oh yes, came the eager reply, we are really going to do it, we are on our way Patti!

Shaking my head, to confirm his positive answer, I said, we will be okay Chris, won't we?

'Course we will, it will be good fun, the biggest adventure we have ever had.

I couldn't help thinking that night, as I tossed and turned in bed, listening to the old grandfather clock striking 3-00 a.m. It all seemed surreal, and as the final days approached, it felt like it was happening to someone else, and I was observing from a front row seat!!

Finally, all we had to do was to say our goodbyes to family and friends for the next six months. Evening dinner parties or drinks with friends were the order of the day. Our special meal with Jackie and Bill at a very exclusive restaurant saw us 'push the boat out' that night. Chris ordered some excellent champagne to toast our bon voyage. Followed by an excellent dinner with plenty of delicious wine to compliment the meal.

The day before our final departure, we put the remaining belongings into the already over loaded motor home. We had recently bought a 'top box' bolted onto the roof of the van; which was full to the top and padlocked.

No turning back now love, Chris remarked as he came back into the house, we are finally off on our adventure holiday tomorrow!!!

Unable to pluck up the courage to drive the van, I volunteer to be the 'right hand man' and map read instead. Over months of planning and chartering our route, I already had a rough guide as to our ultimate directions. Setting off very early, the first day of our holiday, we knew we had most of the day to drive to the port in a leisurely manner. The weather was kind to us, as we cruised along the motorway, enjoying the morning sunshine and the late summer warmth through the windscreen.

Two hours into travelling, I started getting a numb bum, and said to Chris, would it be a

Good idea to pull off the motorway to a 'services station' and stretch our legs and have a cup of tea. Putting the motor home in the designated areas for caravans and motor homes, I thankfully jumped down from my passenger seat and vigorously rubbed both sides of my bottom to get the blood flowing again.

Oh! That's better, I said, now just lead me to a hot steaming cup of tea, 'there's nowt like it' ha ha . . . The restaurant was quite full of touring motorists and families, on the move, travelling to who knows where. Its strange to think of so many people travelling every day, all the time, day and night. Always on the move, be it in cars, trains or planes.

Yes, you are right, came the reply, when you look back to our grandparents, and great grandparents, they seldom moved from their town or village all their lives. How different things are 100 years later.

An hour later after a look round the service station shops, we were back on the motorway and made the decision over coffee to spend the afternoon in the City of York, for lunch and a walk round the beautiful old town to do some sightseeing.

We always know when we are approaching the outskirts of York, as the main road leading into York itself has an elegant tree lined avenue, with many beautiful houses set back behind a leafy vista. Steeped in ancient history, and resulting archaeology, with pretty and unusual shops, cobbled walkways and a wide choice of restaurants. Tourists from all over the world come to enjoy what the City has to offer. There is something there to amuse and delight everyone.

Around the old part of the city, one can usually see ongoing archaeological digs, with an enthusiastic team of youngsters from local universities. The atmosphere in the centre is electrifying with a large cross section of visitors from all over the world coming to absorb the City history. Beautiful hanging baskets, crammed with a colourful variety of summer flowers cascade down the walls of the old shops and commercial buildings. As we stroll through the narrow alleys, we look up to see the exposed timber framed buildings from above. Below, are the bow fronted, jam jar glass bottom windows, which reminds you of the Old Curiosity Shop from the book by Charles Dickens.

We couldn't leave York without visiting a very well known tea room, where it seems, time has stood still in its persistence to keep old fashioned custom and elegance of a bygone era. Waiting to be seated, a pretty young lady dressed in the customary black and white uniform approached us and smiling, she lead us to a crisp white cloth covered table. Comfortably seated, we ordered their well known and delicious afternoon tea.

I love coming here, I said, glancing round the room at the 1930's décor, its so elegant isn't it? A few minutes later, she brought our afternoon tea to the table along with a lovely three tiered cake stand with a colourful assortment of homemade cakes.

This all looks delicious, I said smiling at Chris, and then added, 'shall I be Mother?

We spent the remainder of the afternoon enjoying our tea, but time was marching on. Chris preferred to find the ferry terminal at Hull before nightfall, as we were both unfamiliar with this particular town and ferry port.

Travelling down the A1079 from York, there seemed to be a faint squeak emitting from the back of our motor home, noticeably when he either stopped or pulled away in first gear. Nothing was mentioned at first, but as we progressed towards Kingston upon Hull, the faint squeak became even louder, sounding like a cat caught in the back wheels.

What's that noise, I ventured, as I caught his expression. I don't know, it sounds like the brakes are sticking, but I have checked the handbrake is fully down and depressed my foot brake a couple of times, but nothing seems to work. My stomach started turning over, and I sat there in compete silence as the noise steadily increased. We were nearing the port and pulling onto the car park at the ferry port terminal, Chris jumped out to check at the Ticket Office on the details of our departure later that night.

Are we okay to carry on, the noise on the van seems to be getting worse, I said as we started to join the queue of vehicles. He nodded a yes, and added, 'if we can nurse it along to the family home in Switzerland, we can get it repaired over there'

As we waited to drive on the ferry, I made a cup of tea and packed an overnight case in readiness.

We sat watching the ferry workers inside the large gaping mouth of the boat. Bright strip lights lit up the interior, to reveal metal grips and chains on the deck area. A hugely long and wide gangplank sloping out towards the concreted dockyard, also had metal grips and runners for the safe entry and exit of heavy trucks and cars.

Looks like the queue is moving now Patti. Change the van battery switch over, and make sure all the doors and cupboards are locked, we don't want anything flying out and hitting us on our head.

Oh! No! I exclaimed, the squeaking has started up again. We were gradually being separated from lighter vehicles and motorbikes, to join another queue of lorries and heavy vehicles. Turning the engine of the van off again, we waited to be summons onboard. Some Dutch and Germany lorry drivers were standing apart from their vehicles waiting, and as we approached, a discussion ensued between them. We had wound our windows down to get some fresh air and one of the lorry drivers shouted over to us and pointed to the back wheels of our motor home. With his right index finger stuck out, he began to make circular motions, and grimaced.

Did you see that, I asked Chris, the lorry drivers are trying to tell us the brakes are sticking.

There's nothing I can do now Patti, we will just have to get over to Rotterdam and then see how it is.

It was our turn to board, I felt excited and then scared, getting butterflies in my stomach as one of the ferry men waved us forward to slowly ascend the gangplank until we leveled off inside. He was taken over by another guy who waved and pointed simultaneously, until we were squeezed in behind a very large container lorry. Chains were clanked and metal moved against metal, until we were safely anchored in place for the twelve hour journey. A quick check around the van, pulling all the shutters down, we grabbed our overnight things and jumped out of the van. We were met by a pungent smell of oil, diesel and lorry fumes.

Poo! This smell is making my eyes water, I said as we tried to squeeze past the lorry in front of us to get to the exit door.

Just follow me and watch where you are walking, the floor is very slippy in parts with spillage from vehicles.

We walked to reception to find our room and get the keys. We were greeted by one of the crew members who asked us to follow him down a series of long corridors set out like a rabbit warren.

At this point, dear reader, I must digress once again to let you in on another secret of mine—I very easily get lost!! I have no sense of direction; strange, because I am good at map reading. On foot, totally useless! I remember once in Manchester airport for a holiday in Egypt, a few minutes to go before boarding. I wanted the loo. Chris said, I will wait here for you, but don't be long. I wasn't, and walking out of the door again, I couldn't see him. I wandered about for ages, feeling really upset and worried. In the end, when I heard them calling the flight to go to the gate number, I panicked and thought I'd better find a security man and tell him I was lost!

Chris saw me then, and shouted for me to stop whilst he hurried over. We found out later that I had walked in one door and out though the other side of the toilet block. 'Well, how was I to know they had two identical looking doors, it could have been worse, one of my friends walked into a broom cupboard once thinking it was the exit door.

Back to my story—There is a chart plan of the corridors and corresponding numbers on each of the floors the steward told us as he closed our cabin door.

Admiring the cleanliness of the room, Chris said, 'are you sleeping up on the top bunk bed Patti?

Pulling a face, I replied, I think you already know the answer to that one, dear heart.

We came into the large and brightly lit dining room at 8-30 p.m. after a shower and change of clothes, to find many people already having their evening meal. All along one side of the restaurant was a large variety of delicious food. An assortment of hot vegetables in stainless steel trays, boiled, roast and chipped potatoes. One of the six chefs were systematically carving roast beef and pork to a never ending queue of hungry diners. There was roast chicken and an assortment of fish. Further down was a colourful display of crispy salads and cold meats. Fresh fruit and a mouth watering array of sweets and pudding completed the evening dinner menu.

Our eyes travelled over the beautifully presented food as we waited to be seated. We were shown to a relatively quiet corner of the large dining room. We spent a lovely evening enjoying a leisurely meal. To mark the beginning of our holiday adventure, Chris ordered a chilled bottle of champagne, brought to our table in a silver bucket and placed on a stand nearby.

Oh! I do feel posh, I said as Chris poured the champagne.

Well, that's because we are darling, for tonight at least.

Whew! That was a good meal, I said, leaning back and stretching my overfull stomach.

Do you want to have a look round the boat and walk some of the dinner off, Chris replied.

That's a good idea, I won't be able to sleep tonight otherwise.

The open cul-de-sac area was given over to gambling. A constant click-clack of the roulette ball made us both stop to watch. A number of clients were placing their bets before the croupier, who spun the wheel once again. Nearby, others were engrossed in various card games, organized by a sophisticated young woman with a permanent fixed smile; they gambled at the turn of a card.

Time was marching on as we opened our door to try and get some rest. We had a long day ahead of us tomorrow, but mentioning the constant dull boom of the ships engine below, coupled with spasmodic tannoy announcements, it was going to be quite an eventful night.

We were woken very early next morning by a loud tannoy announcement at 5-00 a.m. telling us breakfast was being served in the dining room prior to docking at

7-00 a.m.

Just a coffee for me Chris I said, I am still very full from the dinner last night.

We will make that two coffee's then and get something to eat later on this morning.

As we drove down the ferry boat ramp, we joined the slowly moving line of traffic proceeding through passport control. We already had a knowledgeable layout of the roads leading out of the port, and through the industrial parts of Rotterdam, as we had previously been over in our car to visit family a few years ago.

I love the straight and flat roads of Holland, and the many straight canals running alongside I said. The old wooden windmills with the sails turning in the wind, greeted us as we drove away from the port.

The brakes were still squealing and protesting as we drove towards our family home in Switzerland. As we intended staying with them for two weeks, we had plenty of time to get the motor home fixed then.

At this point, we started working as a team; Chris concentrating on driving along the auto ban, passing Dusseldorf and Koln. I was concentrating on map reading and directing along our chosen route to Switzerland. We safely reached a beautiful Nature Park just past the town of Bonn for our first over night camp. We had found a lovely site surrounded by a large forest of dense evergreen trees. Suitably ensconced on 'hard standing' so the motor home tyres wouldn't sink into the mud, we were connected up to their electricity with the aid of a continental adaptor. Lovely hot showers and clean facilities, coupled with a hearty evening meal ensured that we both slept soundly and woke refreshed next day.

A jolly good cooked breakfast next morning to keep us going for a few hours, we repacked the van and stowed everything securely away so there would be minimal banging and rattling as Chris drove on. Being hit sharply on the head once before with a couple of flying books when we first bought the motor home, reminded us to check that all the doors and cupboards are locked down before pulling away.

Where are we heading for now Patti, Chris asked me as we drove out of the camp site gates.

I thought we could meander down through the Black Forest, I replied. Do you remember last time we came over here in the car, we did this journey then, its very beautiful. The sunrays were shining through the pine trees onto the damp forest floor below. A strong smell of pine scent wafted through the open window, and a large amount of unseen birds were singing and twittering in the treetops.

What a lovely morning I exclaimed as I poked my head further out of the window to take deep breaths of the scented air and scowl at the persistent noise emanating from the back wheels.

There's that noise, AGAIN!

Stop worrying Patti, it will be fine just as soon as we get to our sons home.

Negotiating the smaller roads down through the Black Forest, we admired the ornately decorated and exposed timber framed houses with bright red geraniums hanging down from wooden window boxes. Old farming equipment was carelessly laid in the yard at the side of a Dutch barn style timber barn. Passing through the pretty Bavarian villages, renown for the clock makers, we saw extremely ornate and detailed wooden cuckoo clocks which were displayed along the roadside. We slowed down to not only drive very carefully through the narrow streets, but to get a lovely moving picture and admire such wonderful craftsmanship.

We were now entering the remarkable village of Villingen on the German/Swiss border. It would appear to have been lost in the mists of time as the whole place had a uniquely Bavarian feel to it. Settled deep in an open green valley, with many vineyards on both sides of the sloping mountains; it would probably be their main source of income, coupled with tourism. We already knew there was a suitable campsite here waiting for us to spend the night. What we didn't know was that they were preparing for a wine-fest in the village over the weekend. As this was late afternoon on a Saturday, we had already seen a large marquee placed in the central square, with a few open sided hot food stand in the process of being set up.

Luckily for us, the site owner had just one available 'hook up' left for two nights, and did we want both? We both nodded agreeably and smiled at the thought of experiencing a German wine-fest. Settled in once again, we both said how lovely the site and the village was, and agreed to do some walking on the second day through the upward slopes of the vineyards.

I think we shall eat out tonight, Chris said, as we had got showered and changed.

We can walk down to the village square and watch the celebrations too. I was talking to the site managers son earlier, and he said, there will be a live band on tonight.

We could hear some 'oompah' music playing as we walked down the road towards the large marquee in the square. 'Doesn't the music sound jolly, I said laughing, they are playing 'Tulips from Amsterdam'—listen!! As we approached, the early revelers were already joining in the fun as we entered the marquee and sat down. The band was suitably elevated on a central wooden platform playing to several couples on the small dance floor. Holding each other tightly around the waist, they were concentrating on doing a fast 'jiggly dance' and bobbing up and down. Trestle tables almost the full length of the room covered the remaining floor space, along with wooden benches where many revelers sat side by side and sang along to the 'oompah' band. The wine tent was situated on the other side of the square with four bartenders serving nonstop to an ever growing queue of people. Chris joined the queue to buy some local wine, shouting over to me above the increasing noise of the music and laughing and talking.

Do you want red or white, he shouted. White, I mouthed back to him grinning. A few minutes later he came back to me and handing me my glass of wine said.

Phew! Its mayhem over there, do you know, they are charging a deposit of one euro on each glass, refunded when you take them back.

How much was the wine then, I enquired.

Only 50 cents a glass, Chris said laughing, the deposit on the glasses were more than the wine!

We walked back to the marquee and found a couple of seats at the end of a row. The bier and wine flowed and the locals got noisier. I watched a large party of guys in their leather lederhosen, sitting together on another table, singing along in a bawdy way to some of the familiar German songs and swaying from side to side in unison. As they held their large bier steins in a clenched fist, a small amount spilt over onto the increasingly wet paper cloth.

Lets go and see what there is to eat, Chris shouted to me above the noise. I am hungry now, are you? Nodding, but not bothering to even try to speak over the din; we got up and walked outside again into the warm evening. There was a variety of delicious and mouth watering smells coming from the food tents. Looking at each one in turn, fried chip potatoes, juicy beef burgers, a locally made bratwurst sausage with fried onions, we chose what we wanted and sat outside under the stars.

Time to go now, Chris said, as he watched me yawning. Its been another long day and a good party.

As we walked into the campsite, the site owners were having a party of their own. It was their daughter's birthday, and the celebrations were in full swing on the pretty outside terrace; lit by multi coloured fairy lights. Waving to us, they called out, 'have you both enjoyed the wine fest tonight?

Yes, we both shouted back, its been really good.

It was the melodious chiming of the little church clock in the village at 7-00 a.m. that disturbed our sleep. Over breakfast, we made the days plans to do a good walk out of the village and up through the vineyards. The previous day when we had arrived, we made enquiries as to some local walks. She said that there is a lovely walk which meanders up through the vineyards, and along the ridge top, with spectacular views of the valley, mountains and pine forests in the distance.

Pulling our boots on and a warm jacket, we set off for the day as soon as we had the breakfast pots washed and tidied away. We immediately found the narrow dirt path leading to the uniformed rows of carefully tended vines. The sun shone, but there was a slow build up of scudding clouds which temporarily blocked the suns warmth as we ascended to the top of the ridge. Eventually reaching the highest point, we paused to catch our breath and look at the panoramic views. Far

Below, was the tiny matchbox village, nestling deep in the basin shaped valley; giving some protection from the harsh winds and snow of the winter month. Rising steeply up on all sides, were the continuous rows of vines, their pendulous fruits hanging in large juicy bunches, ripened with the warm summer sunshine; and waiting to be harvested.

It makes your eyes water doesn't it? It is so beautiful, I said as we continued to tread cautiously along the narrow ridge path. Pausing once more, we looked out

Towards the massive sea of pine trees in the Black Forest, and in the distance the magnificent Swabian Alps.

Its been a fantastic day hasn't it? I said, as we returned to the motor home once again. Pulling off my boots and opening the door I said, I am ready for a nice cup of tea and a rest, what about you?

OUR FAMILY IN SWITZERLAND

As we were already on the German/Swiss border, we knew it wasn't very far to our son's home from the camp site at Villigen.

Telephoning him that morning, we confirmed our approximate time of arrival, before driving out of the village. As we were heading in the general direction of Zurich, the familiar landscapes started to come into view.

Switzerland!!—For those of you who have never been.

It is quite perfect in almost every way. No litter or graffiti. The crystal clear mountain air is startlingly fresh, as the many beautiful lakes and Rhein falls. From the Bavarian open timber beamed houses, we were now looking at the pretty 'chocolate box' Swiss chalets, again, with tumbling waterfalls of bright red geraniums hanging down from their wooden windowsills. Undulating emerald green hillsides rise up, set against the huge mountain ranges, as we journey along to our family's home in their quiet sleepy village. Herds of doe eyed cattle, some with large ornate cow bells around their broad necks, make a constant dull clanging sound as they crop the sweet grass in the meadows.

As we approach their village, my stomach started doing back flips with excitement at the thought of seeing my much loved family. Coming to a stop on their drive, we knocked on the door and looked through the window. We saw our oldest grandson grin back and then shout, They are here, they're here! He rushed to open the door and grasping me around my waist, I bent down to give him a big cuddle and kisses. My word I said, holding him away from me for a moment, 'you ARE growing tall, you will be as tall as your Daddy soon'

Edging thro the door, in a crab like fashion, so as not to hurt him on the door frame. Our youngest grandson came charging down the stairs and launched himself off the bottom two steps shouting 'Nana England, Granddad' at the top of his voice. (Its has never been Nana, always Nana England).

Oh! Darling, I said, holding him tightly to me, and smothering him in kisses, making him laugh. Looking up, our dearest son and daughter in law appeared, and tears of joy flowed freely as we all hugged and kisses each other. The boys bounced round us like a pair of young kangaroos. We spent the rest of the day catching up with all our news. Chris told them that we were having some trouble with the van, and it needed to be checked out before we attempt going over the Swiss alps. They both re-assured us that they could find an experienced garage mechanic who would be qualified to repair it.

By lunchtime, our beautiful daughter in law had everything organized for Chris to drive the motorhome to the garage and start repair work. 'I will go in our car and lead the way, she said, you follow behind me; then we will leave your van and come back together in our car.

I stayed behind to watch over the grandsons. Chris and I had played a game called 'Connect 4' with youngest grandson most of the morning. I think between us both, the adults were losing three to one! Our little sweetheart was only five years old that year!

Nana England—NANA ENG—LAND; Shouted a disembodied voice. 'Come outside and play'. Opening the patio door, my little sweetie was beaming back at me, football in his hands. Nana England, lets play football' Then he proceeded to tell me the rules of the game. Football in the middle of the lawn. One lot of shrubs at the end of the garden, the goal post; the other goal post was the patio.

'Right! He said, when I say GO' and without further ado, he promptly flicked the ball with his foot away from me, and laughing, kicked it hard into the shrubs.

AHhh! I said, we play the game like that huh? He looked puzzled for a moment, before announcing his 1-0 score!

Managing to get up to a 9-0 score in ten minutes, I thought I would level the game scoring, and cheat a bit as well!

Putting MY foot on the ball, I smiled down at him, and with the opening music of 'Match of the Day' on television, TRA LA LA LA—I sang, as I hooked the ball with my toe, and holding his arm gently, I kicked the ball sharply onto the patio. 'GOAL' I shouted, doing a good impression of Wayne Rooney. 'ROO-NEY—ROO-NEY' I shouted, dancing round the garden. IT'S A GOAL!! I sniggered as bent down laughing. 'YOU CHEAT'—I am telling Granddad, he said. Then grabbing the ball, he added, 'That's minus six to you'—HUH!!! WHAT???

Daughter in law and Chris returned later to tell me the van would be in over night and they would telephone when it was ready. After lunch our son asked us if we would like to have a walk. A few minutes later, saw the three of us striding out towards the centre of the village and along to the huge forest beyond. The afternoon was warm and bright under a cloudless blue sky as we held deep conversation, walking three abreast. Coming into the village itself, the local people greeted each other politely and smiled at us.

No wonder you enjoy living over here, I remarked to my son.

It's very clean and a safe place to bring the children up, my son replied. No bullying in the schools either.

We were soon out of the village and had joined the many 'Vanderweg' paths, criss-crossing through the dense forest of pine trees. Our boots crunched on the many layers of fallen pine needles over the years. Complete silence! with only the occasional rustle of a small animal on the forest floor, alerted by our low voices as we passed by. I could smell the familiar scented pine, accentuated by continual dampness. Slowing down, I collected some fallen pinecones to take back with me. My husband has accepted long ago, whilst out walking, I bring back pinecones, small stones and shells, as either ornamentation or instrumental in making mosaic pictures.

In a leafy clearing, set back from the forest, a beautiful young mare was high stepping towards us. Her graceful neck proudly arched, and with large liquid brown eyes, she glanced in our direction as we passed by. Her glossy chestnut brown coat gleamed in the afternoon sunlight, a few moments later, she was gone! Our son told us she would be from the Polo Club further along from here, and sometimes he takes the family down to watch them practice or play in polo matches.

The ten day visit to our little family in Switzerland flew by and it was time to move on, and drive over the St Bernadino Pass and into Italy. Preparations were made to have a fairwell dinner at a lovely Italian restaurant. Our motor home had been repaired and was completely road worthy again. We had played with our little sweetheart, listened to oldest grandson practice his guitar, and talked to him about school and his future. I had read some traditional English stories out to them before bedtime every evening. Picked our youngest grandson up from nursery, and held long conversations with our son and daughter. We had thoroughly enjoyed every minute, but it was time to leave!

I felt sad and upset as Chris and I did our final preparations. More tears fell, as we climbed into our motorhome and drove away. Tooting the horn gently, as a final goodbye, we turned the corner and—we were gone!!

TUNNEL DEL ST BERNADINO PASS

Speeding along on the motorway towards the town of Chur, on the A13, the motor home was behaving beautifully, no loud worrisome squealing, the brakes had been repaired for the next leg of our exciting journey taking us over the St Bernardino Pass.

It was a typical autumn day, with blue skies and warm sunshine, coupled with a sharp nip in the air mid morning. Following directions to the road leading over the Pass, there were a few cars and heavy vehicles in front of us taking the same route. As we approached the Pass, a large sign indicated the 'Pass Closed'—with heavy gates blocking the road to confirm 'no entry'. All traffic was directed instead through the St Bernardino tunnel.

Gradually, the landscape had changed from undulating green pastures this morning, to snow capped mountains and a large continuous line of neat banks of snow, either side of the road; shoveled regularly by industrious snow ploughs. The outside air had changed dramatically too, as we ventured up the steep mountain roads, we adjusted the heating in our motor home to a higher setting.

Eventually, we see in the distance, our road leading through the huge tunnel; hacked through the middle of solid mountain rock. Putting our dipped beam on in the van, we came from bright sunlight into a comparatively long dark tunnel, although the tunnel did have some dimmed lighting either side of the road, coupled with emergency telephones and refuge bays.

We appeared to be driving for ten minutes or so until we saw a glimmer of light coming from the exit of the tunnel. The light slowly grew larger until we came out into the bright sunshine once again. As we got clear of the tunnel traffic, Chris indicated the van to pull over into 'lay by 33'. By now, it was late afternoon at and the natural light was fading. Our intention was to have the added excitement of camping over night, right at the very top of the mountain Pass.

'No electric hook up tonight, no hot showers' Chris remarked, looking out of the window smiling at two young men in their 20's, their car parked next to us, packed to the roof with camping equipment. They were in the middle of a snowball fight and having an icy cold wash as well. Shrieking and laughing at each other, they had stripped to the waist, their bear chests were red with the missiles they were hurling at each other. We both sat watching them fascinated, as the 'fight' went on for a good fifteen minutes. Soaked to the skin and freezing cold, they returned to their car to towel themselves dry.

Do you fancy doing that, Chris said, grinning at me. Trying to think of a sharp answer back and failed. I just shrugged and got up to make the dinner saying, 'you go out first, I'll join you in a minute' HE DIDN'T !!

Over dinner, we watched the sun go down, reflecting light onto the snow peaks, it gave the impression of a warm pink glow. Every window in our motor home had an amazing view, and we kept the blinds open until total darkness fell before we closed them all and locked up for the night.

Next morning, we woke to the sound of occasional vehicles driving by. 'Another bright morning, I said, quickly pulling on my clothes after a 'cat lick' wash' Oh! It's freezing in the van this morning. 'I don't suppose you fancy having a snow bath then Patti? Came the reply.

We were almost ready for moving on two hours later, but I couldn't resist taking a few pictures before leaving. Climbing down the steps from the personnel door, I gasped as the freezing cold morning chill took my breath away and started making me violently shiver. I had forgotten, in my haste, to put a coat on, as the morning sun made it all look very warm and inviting. As I turned back to the door to open it again, I saw Chris laughing at me through the window. 'Go on' he mouthed and urgently waved one hand towards me, 'it's a nice fresh day! Still shivering, I quickly took some photographs and then dashed back to the van and locked the door. Whoa!! It's freezing out there, I said, grabbing my coat and putting it on.

A quick spot check to secure all doors and cupboards, seat belts on, engine turned over, and we were off again!!

'Did you write out the next set of routes, Chris asked, as we started decending down the steep mountain road. It hadn't snowed in the night, but there was still plenty of snow to look at on each side of the road. I said that I had written out the next few stages of our journey, the next point of destination was towards Lugano and Como.

A few years ago, I came over to Switzerland to visit our family. Our son and daughter in law took me out for a really nice day trip to the very pretty town of Como made famous with its centrally situated lake. Its ornamented promenade and walkways ran round the picturesque lake, framed by a series of mature trees. An elegant and prosperous town, with beautiful, but expensive shops. I bought a lovely chiffon scarf, which was graciously deposited in a very smart faux leopard skin bag with chain handles.

Relating this story to Chris, he told me he would do a brief detour to Como and stop a while for some lunch. Unfortunately, we couldn't find a suitable parking place for our motor home, as we have to always consider the length as well as the width; the only drawback, we have found in owning a motor home. The 'park and ride' system in England is brilliant. You can leave your vehicle a few miles outside a town in complete safety. Regular buses run from the park and into the town centres.

It's just as well, Chris remarked, as we re-traced our original route back to the autobahn. We need to get some miles under our belt, and find a nice place this afternoon to park up for the night.

Negotiating the busy ring road round Milan, found us cutting across country towards the North East coast of Italy, passing by many popular major towns and cities.

I do not drive our motor home, but admire anyone who regularly drives heavy vehicles and articulated lorries. Motorists will sometimes see a warning sticker on the back of heavy vehicles stating—IF YOU CANNOT SEE MY MIRRORS. I CANNOT SEE YOU. Cars can sometimes get too close to heavy vehicles, they do not use head mirrors, only side mirrors; unfortunately, the car is rendered invisible!

We left the autobahn for a little while to take the tension away from Chris, constantly keeping up with the fast and heavy traffic. Driving along a wide dual carriageway in similar direction, with open countryside, I kept seeing one or two young women standing motionless at the curbside. Presently, I said, what are they doing, there doesn't seem to be a bus stop for miles, and no houses nearby.

WORKING! Came the monosyllabic reply.

Working at what, I replied, eying up two women with shorts skirts and high heels.

WORKING!—Ladies of the night, or 'of the day' in this case.

DONG!!—The penny finally dropped! Oh! Ugh! NO—really??

Chris started laughing, and pointed to a young lady and a middle aged trucker climbing out from behind a large bush.

Shaking my head in dismay, I declared—TOO MUCH information!

It was getting late afternoon, we needed to start looking for somewhere to park up before darkness fell. Our thoughts shifted to our number one priority, as we still had a long way to go before arriving on the East Coast of Italy. By now, we had returned to the autobahn, and parked on one of the many large service stations to stretch our legs. As we strolled around, we noticed they had a 'motor home service point' Investigating it further, it was a separate area to not only empty our cassette toilet, but it had clean drinking water too. Over a very welcome cup of tea, Chris said, I think we will park here for tonight Patti, I have done enough driving today, and its going dark'. We will put the motor home over by the lorry park with the others, we will be safe there'.

So for the next 3 days I became a 'truckers moll'—ha ha . . . Several times we used the brilliant autobahn service stations in Italy, no charge, and excellent facilities. Apart from the spasmodic clanging, banging and hissing of air brakes, I felt completely safe. After the initial couple of nights of disturbed sleep with constant noise, we both slept soundly.

Oh! Gawd! What is that noise, I said on our first night, and sitting up in bed, focused my eyes on the clock. 'It's 3-00 a.m. Chris, do these

Chris, CHRIS, are you awake?

I AM NOW, PATTI, came the muffled reply from the partially hidden head under the duvet.

Collapsing back with a groan, I dozed on and off until 7-00 a.m. when I gave up all thoughts of going back to sleep.

BRrrr! It's cold this morning, I said, leaping out of bed to put the propane gas on for a coffee and to warm the van.

Once we had cleared and tidied the van's interior and had something to eat, we were looking at the map to select our route for the day. It had taken me a little while to get use to the road and autobahn layout in Italy, as, unlike England, you follow an 'A' and an

'E' road sign. E.g. A1/E35 towards Piancenza. Once I got use that, and the lack of shower facilities of up to three days sometimes, we covered a lot of kilometers to eventually arrive one afternoon at Rosolina Mare on the beautiful North East coast of Italy.

It was late September, and the weather was still kind to us as we were followed the sun, with the very obvious absence of holiday makers.

Where is everyone? I said, as we drove down the deserted road, with lots of empty chalets and caravan sites. Eventually coming to a halt just before the beach, we got out of the van and walked a few yards. It made us feel as if we had come to a 'party' too late, and everyone had gone home! Scratching his head and laughing at my dismay, Chris said, Well, we are here now, end of season or not, and we are staying for at least one night. We both saw the funny side of it later on, as Chris backed the van up to a line of trees, so we faced out towards the narrow road.

'No-one will bother us here, it's totally deserted for miles, Chris remarked.

As daybreak came, we took an early morning stroll along the pale golden sands at the edge of the Adriatic sea, hand in hand, breathing the cool, fresh ozone. Presently, my husband stopped and turning to me said, 'I wanted to show you Venice, it's not very far from here, and we have just over a week before we catch the ferry from Ancona to Patra, would you like to go?

Let me think about it, I said, after a few moments.

Dashing back for our swimming things, we hastily changed into them returning to the sea for an early morning dip. Chris didn't hesitate, he waded slowly in and started calling out to me to follow him. I paddled in the shallows for a while, asking him if the water was very cold.

NO!—It's Luv-er-ly! Come on in!

Here goes, I shouted, and made a sudden dash for it!

It was quite warm still from the long summer months, once you got over the initial shock; then it became similar to taking a warm bath. We had missed having a daily shower for three days up until then, as water was at a minimum on the autobahn stations. So it was a real treat to use the Adriatic as our bathroom.

'What are we doing today Chris, I asked, when we eventually returned to the van to get dried off.

Well, if you don't want to drive up to Venice, we can meander down this coastline for a week or so and just camp on the beach, you choose Patti.

Can we do Venice on the way back to England in February? I believe we can book a ferry from Suda Bay, Crete, and with a two night sailing it will bring us into the port of Venizia early morning.

For the next eight days, we barely moved the motor home, as we lived the life of a pair of 're-tread hippies'. The warm sunshine saw us beachcombing and collecting pretty shells on the soft sands, or taking long walks along the edge of the foaming ebb tides. We would sit on the beach in the early evening, and watch the fiery sun sink slowly down over the Adriatic Sea, a warm breeze caressing our tanned bodies.

Most evenings we would have a BBQ on the beach, with the deliciously fresh Italian food we have previously bought from the lovely seaside towns of Ravenna, Rimini or Cattolica. Always, with a good bottle of Italian wine to help digest our food and toast each other's health. Lying back on the sand, we would look up at the magnificent night sky with thousands of very bright stars, twinkling back at us, set in the backdrop of an inky black sky. Another perfect day had come to an end, as we watched the dying embers of the fire gradually fading away.

One morning, we decided to go into Rimini for a spot of sightseeing and to do some food shopping. Safely parking our motor home a little way from the town centre, we wandered through the very beautiful and picturesque old town.

Oh! No! I exclaimed, stopping suddenly and pointing across to a local guy who was walking close to the walls of shops and commercial buildings, constantly tripping and stumbling over various obstacles on the ground. The poor man was obviously blind, and with one hand stretched forward, the other holding a white cane, tapped it from side to side. He didn't appear to be doing a good job!

AWww! Chris, look, we'll have to go and help him. He's either going to get run over, or fall and break his neck.

I started to walk over to the guy as Chris muttered behind me 'there you go again Patti, always collecting lame ducks'.

I gently took hold of the guy's arm, so as not to startle him, and asked him if he would like some help to cross the busy road ahead.

He smiled and said something in Italian. Chris had caught up by then, and said in a low voice, 'he doesn't understand English, so what are you going to do?

Hesitating for a moment, I managed to save the poor man from doing a par de deaux over a bicycle leaning against the wall. I replied, Well, I'll take him over the road anyway.

A loud tut emanated from my husband's lips from behind me, as I firmly gripped his elbow to steer him towards the curbside. The guy obviously knew where he was going, as he stopped at the curb with me, and muttering something in rapid Italian, pointed over in a general direction of a café with his stick.

Ah! Café, I said, with embellishment, trying to sound like a local, and trying my best to understand him. He nodded back at me anyway.

I glanced behind to look at Chris' face for approval, only to receive a look of dismay and wry amusement.

We are going to the café, I shot back to Chris, with an air of authority.

Opening the door to let my new 'friend' go in first, he tapped his way up to the counter, to be instantly greeted by a nice young man who thankfully for me spoke some English. I had guessed by now, this blind man who I had literally picked up off the street, and insistently brought him down the road, must be wondering who the heck I was!

Introducing ourselves to the amusement of the young barman, I hastily explained that we had seen him trip and almost fall over various things as he was trying to get down the street. Smiling, he said that the guy comes in almost every day for a coffee and a chat. He knows the layout of the roads and his way here he added, and you are not the first person who has helped him into my café. He is regularly picked up by tourists who have also seen him stumbling and brought him in here.

Well, I never, I said, laughing and looking at Chris, who had that look of 'I told you so' on his face.

He wants to buy you both a coffee, the barman said, by way of thanking you. So we spent another half an hour drinking his strong black coffee and having a chat, with the barman acting as interpreter

That was nice, I said to Chris, as just the two of us walked back down the road to get our food shopping. 'It was our good deed for the day'. HMmmm! Came the reply, as Chris pointed to a large motorbike speeding past us on the road, with our blind friend riding pillion on the back!!!

We had moved our motor home to a particularly lovely stretch of beach further along the coastline. As darkness was falling the sky was lit up with our usual heavenly host of stars. Our added bonus being, that tonight was a big bright full moon! As always, we had left the blinds undrawn so we could gaze out of the front windows at the night sky.

Look at that lovely big moon, I said; looking up, shall we have another BBQ on the beach tonight?

Initial preparations were made to spend our evening outside, and enjoy the moon and stars, the warm sand and the soothing noise of the waves as they rushed to shore. It was nearing the end of our unique seven day holiday on the beach; soon we would be sailing over to mainland Greece and pursuing the onward journey towards our villa in the foothills. But tonight, there would be good food and wine, laughter and romance on our beautiful deserted beach in the moonlight.

Chris soon got the BBQ coals lit and smoldering away nicely, he collected some driftwood nearby to build a campfire. Meanwhile, I prepared a salad, and gave the meat a generous coating of BBQ spices. Then wrapping some large potatoes in tin foyle, to be put in the coals later on; all there was left for me to do was to put some music on. With a bit of thought and careful negotiations to avoid getting sand in our food, we sat round the campfire to enjoy our evening meal with a chilled bottle of Italian wine.

CHEERS!! We said in unison, stin-e-yammas!

Shall we dance? I said, getting up and holding my hand out for Chris to join me. We strolled down towards the gentle incoming tide, still brightly lit by the moon. Listening to the soft music coming from inside the motor home, and drawing me close into his arms, we slowly danced together in the shallow waters of the Adriatic sea. It was well after midnight by the time we went inside again. Chris had damped both fires down and collected all our rubbish up. This was to be our last evening at the seaside, as by late afternoon next day we would be driving toward the ferry port of Ancona, to board the boat bound for Patras on mainland Greece.

What does this 'camping onboard' facility entail I asked next morning over breakfast.

From what the shipping line has told me, Chris replied, we pay slightly less money for the trip over to Greece, as we will not require a cabin. We will sleep in our motor home instead and have use of their showers and toilet facilities. Electric hook up is available too if we want to use it.

Will we all be together with other vehicles on board or on our own, I enquired?

We'll be separated from the passengers who have cars, as they will drive them on and leave them locked up to sleep in one of the cabins until next day. We will be one floor above the car deck, on a semi open area, Chris replied.

Ah! That's good then isn't it? We WILL be fastened down securely again, won't we? I'd hate to shunt forward suddenly when we are in bed, and shoot out across the floor.

Don't worry, they will probably put chocks under the wheels of all the heavy vehicles or if the sea is rough, put chains around the wheels.

I was re-assured and happy, as I settled back to look at the lovely scenery as we sped along to Ancona. Four thirty p.m. came round, and as we watched through the front windows of our motor home, the long queue, which we had joined earlier in the day, began moving. In single file, the vehicles were being directed once again, up the ramp and into the huge aperture of the ferry boat. We were waved over to the opposite side of the ramp, right behind a dark green Volkswagen campervan. The vehicle plates told us that they hailed from Germany. There appeared to be two adults and three children inside. Whilst we had been stationary, we watched in amusement, as Mother got out and walking to the van of the Volkswagen, she opened the storage boot.

Wow!! I said in amazement, as we both stared at the boot packed up to the roof with clothes, bedding, food and camping equipment. She sure knows how to pack things in every available space.

Chris started laughing, and said, I wonder where they all sleep? Do you think they take turns and sleep in rotation, or stack the kids one on top of the other?

Don't let her see you are laughing at them, for goodness sake I said, trying my best to keep control, as I felt a good belly laugh coming on.

It was our turn to board, and as we carefully watched for directions, we were directed to park right behind the green Volkswagen, with one side of our van right up against the open railings of the boat. Spending the remains of the day, we had a long hot shower, most welcome after bathing in the sea for a week. By now, we were fast running out of clean underwear and desperately needed to wash some of the growing pile of dirty clothes. We both took some underwear with us to the showers, dropping them on the floor of the shower tray to wash them at the same time as we washed ourselves. Returning back to the motorhome, I hung my knickers out over the wing mirrors to dry, with the bath towel draped on the half open window nearest to the boat rails.

Oh! That's good, I remarked, as I watched my knickers and Chris' socks gently blowing in the sea breeze. The towel will be nice and freshly dried too in a couple of hours

An hour later, we returned to our motor home to discover that three pairs of my knickers had taken flight and jumped overboard, never to be seen again? Or maybe not! If you are walking on a beach off the Adriatic coast, and three pairs of pink cotton knickers have been washed up—you'll know they are mine!!

I've got a big surprise for you tomorrow Patti, Chris said, after we had returned to our van for the night. My stomach started doing somersaults again, as I cautiously asked; what is the surprise, not too scary is it?

When we dock at Athens tomorrow, I'm driving towards the city to look for a campsite in the suburbs. The surprise is that I am taking you to see the Acropolis in Athens!!

I couldn't contain myself, and throwing my arms round his neck, I gave him a big hug and kiss. AWw! Thanks love, you know I have always wanted to see the Acropolis and visit Athens. I won't sleep tonight; I am too excited at the thought of going.

But I did!! And next morning, very early, we disembarked in the same structured order as when we first boarded. We soon left the port of Patras behind and followed the road signs toward the city of Athens. It appeared to be easier than I first thought it would be, as I directed Chris onto the E65/8A, Athens/Korinthos road, which followed the coastline.

We were getting nearer to the city, as I started looking for a campsite I had seen in our Caravan and Camping book. The gradual build up of heavy traffic increased somewhat, as the two lane dual carriageway turned into a six lane carriageway. With a central reservation in the middle, there were also six lanes leaving Athens as well. I had almost forgotten to look for a site, as Chris was concentrating fully on the large amounts of vehicles speeding past us. Not wanting to break his concentration, and too nervous to look away from vehicles passing us on both sides; I began to wish that we would see a campsite shortly. Ten minutes later, my wish came true as Chris shouted, 'there's a campsite over there'. It was on the other side of the carriageway! As we sailed past, Chris said, we are in the wrong lane now, I need to move over to the lane nearest the central reservation and wait until I can do a u.turn.

Right, I said, RIGHT!! And feeling sick with a churning stomach, I wound my window down, then sticking my head out, shouted, SLOW

DOWN!! And for good measure, my left hand shot out and I frantically waved it up and down. Amazingly, they did! Whether from good manners or shock at what I did, I don't know, but it worked!!

OKAY! I shouted to Chris, feeling very much in command, Go NOW, they are letting you go. So he signaled and moved across over to the correct lane, to do a u.turn when the opportunity presented itself. Phew!! I said, that was scarey stuff, my knees are knocking together.

It wasn't long afterwards that the most welcome u.turn came into view, and thankfully we were on the right side of the six lane carriageway, nearest to the curb edge looking for our campsite. Chris had approximately timed it when we first saw the site, and told me we needed to drive for about 10 minutes to where the site was situated.

It's There, the campsite sign, it's there, I shouted excitedly, bouncing up and down in my seat. Signaling into the broad leafy driveway, we came to a halt, at last, outside a small office. I stayed in the van to watch Chris get down from the cab and disappear inside the office.

'Please let there be some empty pitches I said to myself, or we will be wild camping again tonight without hot shower facilities.

Chris came out a few minutes later, grinning at me and said he'd booked us in for two nights.

Hurray, that's brilliant, I said getting excited again.

He told me later that the site manageress had given him some information on how to get to Athens and the Acropolis. We catch the bus from over the road opposite the campsite gates to the railway station, and then catch a train or trolley bus to the centre of the city. She gave me a map as well in case we got lost, with the name of the campsite and district too.

I started laughing at her Motherly considerations, which brought back memories of my own Mother tying my dinner money in the corner of my handkerchief when I was in infant school.

We spent the late afternoon, recovering from our ordeal and walking around the pretty campsite amongst the mature woodland trees, to stop suddenly when we both spotted a large black squirrel dart quickly up one of the trees.

Was that squirrel black, I said, or have I started hallucinating with all the excitement of getting here?

No, you are not hallucinating, I saw it too, but I didn't know black squirrels existed.

Early morning, next day, saw us up, washed and ready for the big day ahead. I eventually fell into an exhausted sleep the night before, as I was so excited at the thought of going to Athens. Giving a cheery wave to the manageress we walked down the driveway and onto the pavement at the busy main road.

The early morning commuter traffic occupied all twelve lanes as we stood in awe, our eyes focused on the bus stop over the other side of the road. Teetering on the very edge of the curb, my hand clasped tightly into Chris' hand, my stomach started doing its acrobatic somersaults again! I don't like this, I exclaimed loudly, as we both looked towards the fast oncoming traffic hurtling along the

'When I say GO! Run quickly, when there is a break in the traffic, Chris said.

GO!!!

We made a dash for it, only to get across the first three lanes, and turning our heads towards a young man driving his car towards us, he had the look of a startled rabbit caught in car headlights.

'He's not going to slow down, I said panicking!

Fortunately, Chris made a split second decision, and seeing a temporary break in the traffic behind us, dragged me back to the curb again.

AW!! That was terrible, I said, as I began shaking with fear.

Come on Patti, we will have to try again; the bus will be here soon.

Once again, we teetered at the curb edge and waited.

NOW!! My husband shouted, and pulled me sharply to him as we both ran for our lives across the first set of six lanes to the central reservation.

I felt the blood drain from my face, as we stood amidst the sea of cars and lorries hurtling past us in a manic fashion, to keep their morning appointments.

Now, the next six lanes Patti, we are nearly there!

Quickly! Grabbing my hand again, we both ran and thankfully covered the remaining six lanes to almost collapse on the pavement by the bus stop.

Out of breath, and panting furiously, I was temporarily rendered speechless (unusual for me). Eventually, we had both recovered enough to discuss the diatribes of manic road users.

Oh! Look, the bus is coming, I said. Putting our arm out the bus began to slow down, at the same time, opening his front, middle and back doors. The guy who was waiting at the bus stop with us, dashed to one of the doors and jumped on. As we presented ourselves at the front door of the bus nearest the driver, he looked at us and promptly closed all the doors and indicating, joined the fast river of traffic. Still angry from our last encounter with the mad drivers, I banged on the door shouting. HEY! HEY! At the top of my voice! But totally ignoring us, he went.

Well, I said, WELL!! He was RUDE——he ought to be reported for doing that!

We were probably not quick enough for him, did you see that young man run and jump on the bus? We will have to do that when another bus comes. We are not use to City life. The next bus arrived

10 minutes later, and to ensure we caught that one, I think we both started running towards the bus as he started indicating to pull in.

Well, that was a trial, I said, sinking thankfully down into my seat and watching the continual streams of traffic whizzing past us. Our next stage of the journey was to catch the trolley bus outside the railway station; but we didn't know where we had to get off the bus or how far the railway station was! We will just have to keep a careful watch for a building which looks like a railway station, Chris stated.

Oh! Gawd! I thought to myself, here we go again! I knew the Greek word for train its treno, how hard can it be?

Well, it DID work out quite well actually, because as the bus pulled over to let some passengers off, I spotted the large station outside. Jumping up quickly, I called AFTO, (here) at the top of my voice, just in case this driver was like the other one and drove away. As we watched the bus pull away, we had to start looking for the trolley stop to take us into the centre of Athens.

Where to now, Chris, I asked looking round at the busy streets and the large amount of pedestrians walking quickly by us! Everyone seems to know where they are going, except us! I added.

Now then Patti, this is where our surrogate Mother comes into her own, he replied, she has already told me to walk over the road and catch either the trolley bus or the metro, both will take us into the centre, and where we want to be.

Good old MUM, I said, smiling happily, 'let's go for it'.

'Clang, clang, clang, went the troll-ee. Ding, ding, ding, went the bell. I sang to myself, as we gently rocked from side to side, the trolley bus picking up speed.

Waves of excitement rolled over me as I stared out of the window at the constant hustle and bustle of the City. Eventually coming to a stop, we got out and watched the trolley bus roll away towards another part of the city.

We must have looked like a pair of naïve, hillbillies, as a big local guy sidled up to us and said 'Are you lost?

Chris never uses the word 'lost' in his vocabulary. If we are out walking on the hills and fells of England, or walking in the mountains and gorges of Crete—then we could 'lose our way'

We are lost Chris, admit it, I would say.

No! We have just temporarily missed our way, he will reply.

This was how he replied to this very streetwise Athenian.

'I am not selling these maps of the City, just handing them out to tourists like you, he said. Where do you want to go?

Moments later, saw us walking towards the Temple of Zeus, and laughing at our mistaken dilemma. Along the pavements and towards the park where Asian street merchants illegally selling cheap toys and whilst one sat on the floor to demonstrate; his companion kept a watchful eye for the police. Without warning, the guy on the floor jumped up at the sound of a piercing whistle and hastily throwing the toys in his case, dived into the park and behind some trees until the police car drove by. We were both amused, and agreed that, no matter where you go in the world, you would always see a similar

Arriving at last, to the famous Syntagma Square, the magnificent Temple dedicated to Zeus, King of the Olympian Gods, rose before us. In the sixth century BC, construction work began during the rule of Athenian tyrants; but it remained incomplete until the second century AD, when additional work was carried out under the Roman Emperor Hadrian, some 638 years later. Known to be the largest temple in Greece, its completed magnificence was short lived after invading barbarians pillaged the temple and left it to fall into ruins. As we walked round the temple, the huge towering magnificence was still very apparent to us, and one could easily imagine how marvelous it must have been when it was an important temple all those years ago.

Moving along, we took instruction from our City map and headed towards the Acropolis at the very heart of Athens. As we approached, we were joined by many other visitors from all over the world, making the same pilgrimage slowly up the gradual incline. The walkway had pretty paved areas, and extensive parkland. Buskers and street traders were dotted here and there, giving it a carnival feel to our approach. The atmosphere was high in expectations and good humoured congeniality as we saw our very first view of THE most spectacular Acropolis ever!!

Bringing us to an immediate stop, we gazed in awe.

It was much larger and a lot higher than we had expected. Set against the lovely blue skies, with some scaffolding for the continuous restoration and repairs. We were amazed to see so many people here in late autumn, listening to a few words in different languages as we continued our way up to reach the very top. Pausing now and then to catch our breath, we gazed down over the City of Athens and beyond.

Eventually reaching the Acropolis itself, we were totally amazed to find there wasn't an entrance fee! Large information boards giving details descriptions were strategically placed along the undulating paths.

The Acropolis was originally built on a huge flat topped piece of rock with a height of 490ft—150m, above sea level. Some early artifacts found, were dated to the middle Neolithic period, but other documentation states it could have been as early as the sixth millennium BC. As with any ancient monuments, many countries have invaded over a period of time and placed their individual mark on the Acropolis. Extensive damage has occurred through wars, religion, and earthquakes. It is only now, in the 21st century, that this magnificent work of art can be left in relative peace to be restored to almost its original state.

My favourite place of the Acropolis was the impressive Amphitheatre. Situated part way up, and fully restored, we had paused briefly to look over the stone wall towards the City, almost matchbox in its size. The Amphitheatre, built in a huge open topped bowl shaped area, the semi circular marble seating, gradually descending from the top towards the stage. At the far side was a large stage, where players would have re-enacted their popular theatre productions of the day. At each side of the stage, two large ornately carved marble pillars stood as sentinels, where the players would have been concealed to eventually emerge onto the stage and take their part.

As I sat down and gazed over the wall down below, I could imagine all the local people lounging on the marble seating in their toga and sandals. The ladies would have their hair elegantly coiled up and dressed, Grecian style. Some of the men would wear a halo of laurel wreath on their head. All, would be laughing and talking and waiting, expectantly, for the actors to take centre stage. The play would begin, it would be a popular topic of the day or a famous and much loved part of Greek mythology. I let my thoughts run riot for a few moments, musing on how a 'day in the life' might have been.

We were at the Acropolis for a few hours in the hot sun and hardly any shade. Wandering around from one magnificent building to another until, tired and thirsty we reluctantly decided to come away, and catch our transport back to the campsite.

Next morning, we still felt jaded from our exciting and busy day, and thought we would have a relaxing walk from the campsite. We saw a large park, across a relatively quiet road from the one near our site, with a large amount of deciduous trees at the double gated entrance. As we approached, there was a small security booth with an elderly gentleman inside. Asking permission to enter, he waved us in, smiling. Along the pleasant leafy avenue of trees, formal gardens were displaying a colourful selection of summer plants. A few other local people were either strolling in the sunshine, or sitting on the conveniently placed park benches. As we walked further into the interior of the park, the dense amount of trees gave way to open grassed areas and as we turned down a narrower road, a large austere building came into view.

Uncertain as to which way we should go, the decision was taken out of our hands, when a voice behind us said 'Hello'. We turned to see a very elderly gentleman in a wheelchair, taken out for some fresh air by a young man in a white coat. 'Hello' I replied, bending forward a little and smiling back at him.

In conversation, he said he was born in Germany, and settled in Athens after the war when he married an Athenian woman. He had lived at this hospital for many years, being totally unable to walk; he looked forward to getting out in the hospital grounds for some fresh air. By then, we were including the young hospital worker into the conversation. He said that this hospital was financed by a private trust and donations from various charities; but it was very difficult to keep the place running as it needed so much repair work and modern medical equipment. We also house mentally ill patients here too, but they won't bother you if you see them in the hospital grounds.

'I AM sorry, I replied, we both thought it was just an ordinary public park, we asked the security man at the gate if it was okay to come in, and he said yes'

Smiling at us both, he replied, It IS alright to come in to the grounds. Then pointing to the man in the wheelchair added, 'You have certainly made his day, he doesn't have visitors to come and see him'.

We spent the rest of our time at the campsite cleaning, re-packing and preparing our motor home for the onward journey to Peraias, sailing to Suda Bay in Chania, Crete. Chris had booked our tickets on the previous ferryboat as they had a wi fi connection. This was also useful to keep regular contact with family and friends. 'It isn't too far away from here,' Chris remarked, as we were almost ready to drive onto the six lane carriageway again. 'But I would feel a lot happier today if we could find the port this afternoon, so we will not be under any pressure later on tonight'. Waving a brief goodbye to the site manager, Chris expertly swung the steering wheel over, and the motor home merged with the fast traffic.

I knew the approximate route towards Peraias docks, via the town of Megara. We picked the road signs up for the port; soon we were approaching the stark ugliness of industrial dockland. Parking the van in a relatively quieter area, we relaxed and made a meal before boarding later.

As we settled down in our cabin on the boat, we both agreed that we just wanted to get over to our villa and enjoy the sunshine and laid back way of life. The smooth crossing and subsequent docking routine went without a hitch, and early morning saw us driving away from Chania and onto the familiar road of Crete. Cruising along the coast road, we were impressed at the very beautiful sunrise over the sea, with a promise of a lovely day.

At Last, we had arrived at our villa in Agia Triada! To begin a new chapter in our life, to enjoy many different experience in the not too distance future. I will share them with you!!

CHRISTMAS AND NEW YEAR IN CRETE

Never being away from home before at Christmas, much less, celebrating the festive season in another country; everything felt very strange and very different. We already know the Greek people are religiously devout, so it was unique to be included in their festive celebrations.

A similar pattern like England, unfolds in the run up to Christmas Eve, with all the shops in Rethymnon gaily decorated and lit up. Families visit each other in their homes or eat together in the many restaurants in the towns. An air of excitement was in Rethymnon, when we came to do our Christmas shopping. The large church in the centre of Rethymnon was beautifully decorated outside the open doorway, with large displays of fresh flowers and ribbons; to welcome everyone into their opulent church for the Christmas service. The Nativity of Christ' birth, decorate a few street corners, with a large open sided wooden stable, and figurines of Mary, Joseph and baby Jesus, centrally placed. The three wise men and various sheep and cattle arranged in semi circular fashion. Lit up at night with a bright star, it looked very festive.

We soon settled into a pleasant routine, and managed to get some walking done as well. The weather was still good with dry and sunny weather in the daytime, to go colder at night, with good clear skies. It was then we decided to get some oil for the central heating and began to collect driftwood off the beaches for a fire in the hearth. Weekly visits to the open market in Rethymnon began, and as we bought our regular fruit and vegetables, we also bought the seasonal chestnuts to roast in the fire at night; along with potatoes to bake in the embers. As we became regulars at the market, we got to know Georgie the Orangeman. A friendlier guy you could ever wish to meet. Always happy and smiling, and with limited English and limited Greek, we would pass the time of day and buy his home grown oranges for our 'juicer'.

Spending Christmas Day at a friends house some distance away. They had also invited several other people who were ex-pats to enjoy one of the best Christmas Day's we have had. The settled weather didn't break until after the New Year, consequently, we regularly wore tea shirt and shorts, and even did a bit of sun bathing on Boxing Day, reclining on in our sun chairs on the patio, with a glass of chilled champagne in one hand and a good book in the other!

A party at the local tavern was organized by our friends and the ex-pat community to celebrate New Year. The arrangement was, we would all make some food to bring along on New Years Eve. Extended tables running along the back wall were already full with a huge amount of food, as we put our offerings down. We had made two large pork pies, one with boiled eggs inside, and both were jellied from a rendered down pigs foot which had been continuously boiled for hours on our stove!

The party was in full swing! Our seated tables being colourfully decorated with hats and party poppers, balloons and streamers. 1960's and 70's music played as we got up to dance and join in the fun. Some local Greek people had wandered in and watched, fascinated, as we did a silly dance, with various animated expressions, popular at that time of year.

We had been told ahead of the party that it was customary to celebrate ALL the ex-pat countries and welcome in the New Year! We were the first from England, and we all got up to form a circle to sing 'Auld Lang Syne', watched with fascination by the local Greek people. Then it was the turn of the ex-pats from Belgium, Germany and Dutch countries, who in their turn, sang and danced to welcome their New Year. Last, but by no means least, was the locals turn. They too formed a circle, and danced to a lively piece of Greek music. It was well after 3-00 a.m. by the time we walked (staggered) home to bed further down the road.

CHAPTER 6
GEORGIA'S TAVERA, AGRIMOURI VILLAGE

2nd JANUARY 2011

We decided to go up into the mountains, and walk the excesses of Christmas and New Year. A fine drizzle had set in, and the watery sun appeared now and again as we climbed up towards the village of Agrimouri, nestling in a tiny hamlet with a panoramic view of Georgiapoli fishing village, surrounded by a beautiful mountain range.

Parking the car near the little white church, we quickly donned our walking boots and waterproof coats, to climb further up the rocky hillside at the back of the village. It was very steep in parts, with the absence of well used paths, only goat tracks. Large amounts of wild herbs, their strong pungent smell made stronger by the damp morning air. The sun beams broke through the heavy clouds over the mountains, and shone through the clouds like silver arrows onto the lush green olive groves far below. Sheep and goats grazed on the rocky outcrops, unperturbed by our heavy footfall on the limestone rocks; as we carefully picked our way on somewhat slippery surfaces.

Eventually, we reached the very top of the steep hillside, and paused to look at the 360 degree view, despite the heavier rain, the views were still breathtaking. Turning sharp left onto a newly made path, we walked along the top of the ridge, and noticed many wild flowers coming into bloom. Deep blue lupins, nestling amongst the rocky outcrops for shelter. Tiny violets with their broad dark green leaves, were dotted here and there. Deep orange marigolds, with wild sage and mint leaves were apparent as we continued along, admiring the huge misshapen limestone rock set amongst them.

We passed by a semi derelict hamlet, some houses were still occupied and had small pots of brightly coloured geraniums outside their door. Others had fallen into dereliction, the roof beams were still visible, and held up the remains of the decaying roof. Pausing to look for a moment at a natural well, and an old bread oven inside one of the ruined houses, used regularly many years ago; but now neglected and forgotten. We continued to follow the blue wayfarer mark and began to slowly decend down the other side of the hill on a goat herders path.

We had previously noticed an old whitewashed village taverna in Agrimouri before we began our walk, and decided to go and see if it was open. The weathered door of the taverna was slightly ajar. Stepping inside, I called 'yassas' (hello) and an elderly lady came through from her living area to greet us. Friendly and smiling, she pulled two chairs out for us to sit down at a small paper cloth covered table. Chattering away in rapid Greek, we realized she didn't speak any English at all! I always carry my Greek phrase book, and along with my limited learning of the Greek language, I can usually make myself understood.

In carefully pronounced Greek, I asked for a beer and a white wine. 'Oxi' (no) she said, shaking her head, and muttering something about cold weather, she disappeared behind a well-stocked bar, bringing back with her two tall glasses of rich ruby coloured red wine;

along with some thick slices of home made cake. Then she promptly pulled out another chair for herself and sat down heavily on it and gave me a big smile. The red wine was really good and warmed our stomach, as she had promised it would. Glancing round the room as we ate, it looked very careworn and in need of re-decorating. Old curtains hung, pinned up with nails at the rotting wooden windows. Ornamental trivia on the back wall was thickly festooned with cobwebs, and a few home grown gourds hung suspended from the roof of the taverna.

Slowly we got into a friendly conversation with her as she told us her name was Georgia. Her husband had died a few years ago and she was on her own now, with no family to speak of. She said she grew all her own fruit and vegetables in her little garden, and also had a few hens for regular fresh eggs. On our second glass of red wine, she brought us some of her olives, tomatoes and thick crusty bread. All either grown or made by her in Agrimouri. Between the three of us, we had a lovely afternoon talking together in general chit chat. I asked her if she had a boyfriend! To which she replied, Oh! No! one man was enough, I am content, I have my coffee and my television. But later pointed to her TV in the corner of the room, with a poor reception, and told me in animated conversation that the aerial signal was no good.

Have you any children, she said. I told her that we had one married son living in Switzerland and two grandchildren. What about you Georgia? Shaking her head solemnly, she told us that she had problems years ago, and couldn't have any. Then her face lit up again and continued, 'my mother had nine children, and emphasizing the amount, held all nine fingers up for me to count; then she started laughing again.

Suddenly, she sprang to her feet, and picking a light bulb up from a shelf nearby, and muttering, she toddled off behind the bar area. With a loud scraping of a chair hidden behind the large stack of dried rusk and breadsticks; she hovered over the chair in readiness to climb up and change the light bulb, glancing over to Chris at the same time. 'I think she wants you to volunteer to change her bulb' I whispered. This time, Chris jumped up and waving his hand at her to stop, he stood on the chair himself. As he reached up and vigorously screwed the light bulb into the old suspended light fitting, Georgia shouted Sega, sega, (slowly, slowly) incase the whole lot came off in his hands. Turning the light switch on, to make sure it still worked, satisfied, she returned to her seat producing a lipstick which she handed over to Chris and gesticulated for him to take the top part off. Try as he might, he couldn't get the top of the lipstick off, and she motioned for me to try, with the same result. Resigning herself to the situation, she stood up once more and ambled into the kitchen to return with some more food. This time, it was toasted bread with a liberal sprinkling of sea salt and herbs.

'It's going dark Patti, Chris whispered, and we need to be down off the mountain roads very soon'. I asked Georgia if we could pay her and be on our way, and struggling to her feet once more, went behind the bar to bring us two smaller glasses of red wine. 'Meeso grasse' (some wine) she said smiling again. Meaning 'one for the road' to us.

Oh! Heck! Chris exclaimed, we are going to be here all night at this rate'. We stood up to put our wet coats back on, and asked her again, how much we owed her. She looked at us for a moment, and then looked away slightly embarrassed to say it was five euro's.

'For all this Georgia, surely not' I cried. She looked confused as if she had asked for too much money, and promptly pulled a large orange out from under her apron to give me.

Thanking her profusely, we left her eight euro's instead, and friendly hugs and kisses were duly exchanged, with the promise that we would come back again to see her.

As we drove past the open door of her taverna, with the darkening skies, Chris tooted his horn and I frantically waved and shouted to a broadly smiling Georgia as she waved back and shouted yassas to us.

CHAPTER 7
ANCIENT ELEFTHERNA

NOVEMBER 2010

Continuing down the stony track away from Arcadi Monastry which we had visited earlier in the year. We headed towards the ancient tenth century BC Eleftherna, still one of the most important archaeological sites in Crete if not in Greece.

The weather continued to bless us with warm sunshine and cornflower blue skies as we slowly drove through the lush green olive groves, dotted here and there with orange and lemon orchards. Abundant with wild flowers throughout the year, we see wild cyclamen, violets, marigolds and lupins, amongst rocky outcrops and a bright yellow carpet of clover flowers under the olive trees in the groves.

Parking the car near the start of the walk, we pulled our walking boots on and a light coat with our rucksack already packed. We turned to look behind us as a local village man was walking towards us at a steady pace.

'Yassas' he shouted loudly, as he reached us, and with a wide grin he revealed a set of brown stained teeth! His eyes screwed up against the glare of the sun, extended his hand out to me and shook it warmly. 'Yas' I said, uncertain of what was coming next.

He nodded furiously, and told us his name was 'Minos'—and he would be our guide for the day! We looked at each other and then at the retreating back of Minos in his shabby blue jacket, faded and worn through many years of use as a goat herder. His trousers were baggy and well worn too, giving the impression that they had not seen soap and water for some time. His shoes were a black slip-on type, totally unsuitable for walking on rocky paths and steep hillsides.

Beckoning us to follow him as we reached a path leading down into the valley below, he shouted once again, 'Come, come now, I will show you it all'. He continued at a steady pace with two confused tourists following behind in his wake!

'Here we go again Patti, you seem to attract these characters'. 'I have a new name for you, its Stanley!—as in 'another fine mess you have got me into Stanley' (popular quotation from Laurel and Hardy).

After a few minutes of following Minos, we came to the Byzantine Tower, rising on a north pointing ridge between two streams, with sheer drops on either side. Built originally as a look-out defensive for the ancient Acropolis, its crumbling ruins are still magnificent at what must have been a successful stronghold. It was their that Minos introduced himself properly, all the while grinning back at us and asking our names as well.

My husband said that his name was George (the Greek people don't understand his second name Chris, so its easier to go by his first name George) and this is Patrizia,(my English name is Patricia, but again, there is no sound of SH—as in shut, in the Greek alphabet, so

Patrizia it is here). Next thing I know, he starts embarrassing me by saying how beautiful I was, going into over the top raptures about me. Then, grabbing hold of my hand, started kissing it! My mouth dropped open, and I glanced at Chris who was looking equally astonished!

Thinking to myself, oh goodness me, don't get any nearer, as I started getting a strong whiff of the goats he looks after.

Politely, I pulled my hand away, and giving him a watery smile, I asked him about the tower. Minos sat down and pulled out his cigarettes and lit one. Puffing away contentedly he stared out into middle distance giving us a chance to look round and recover from his amorous outburst!

Ten minutes later, he jumped up and said 'Oh! Patrizia, oh beautiful! Come now with me'. At this point, I didn't know whether to go or take to my heels and run back to the car. Instead, I looked over to Chris, who had a very amused look on his face, and said quietly,'Go on Patti, follow your boyfriend'. Shrugging and shaking my head, I continued to follow the retreating Minos onto the next point of interest. Expecting him to drop further towards the very bottom of the valley and to the Roman rock cisterns, which we had seen the last time we were there. Minos pointed up the hill onto a very narrow goat track with a steep drop on the left side, and beckoned for us to follow him.

Rounding a sharp bend and coming into view was the remains of a very beautiful little church set on a brow of the hill surrounded by many wild herbs and flowers. Minos told us it dated from the Minoan period 2000-1700 BC, and motioned us to look inside. As we did so, he sat down once more to light another cigarette up and wait for us. Stepping over the deep curve of the stone threshold, worn smooth over centuries of local worshippers. The inside walls still had the partial remains of religious paintings. Carved stone and old

Greek writing was still visible. Shortly after, Minos came inside and asked us if we had any children. I replied, that we haven't got any children, as I thought it would be an easier conversation by saying no! Well, it wasn't!

He kept repeating, in trilling tones, that 'if we wanted babies, no problem here'. I didn't really understand that one, so I shall leave this conundrum to you, the reader. Needless to say, I didn't feel very comfortable about it. In the end, it became a battle of will, as we both ignored him and he eventually shut up.

Off we went again, down the steep incline to where we were and following the single track once again along the ridge. Eventually, we came to the very beautifully excavated site of ancient Eleftherna. Well worked and cared for by archaeologists for the last few years, we admired how much work had been done in restorations. Marching up to the gated fence, Minos opened the rickety wire and waved us in. He was useful in his accurate information regarding the excavated site, and said that he had done some digging here to help move the top layers of soil. Originally built by the Minoans, it was occupied by the Roman invaders later, and more building work was put on top of the Minoan structures, which resulted in deep excavation work. Minos walked very nimbly across the tops of the Roman walls which were narrow ledges of about two foot wide, with a six foot drop at either side. He pointed out the remains of the Roman bath houses, and the remains of the centrally situated church. Many foundations of fireplaces, interior walls and stone carving could be seen as we wandered around the site. We noticed a very large old tree growing out from the ancient ruins, its roots deep beneath the stonework of a building.

Glancing across at Minos, he was lighting another cigarette up and shouted over to us asking if we liked the Acropolis. 'Yes, very much, we called back, as we had somehow missed it the last time we were here. Closing the gate again to keep the goats from wandering in. He grabbed my hand and pulling me along with him said, 'Oh! Patrizia, lovely lady, you come now with me Patrizia'. I looked over my shoulder to see Chris trying to hold a good belly laugh in, his face screwed up in concentration of not making a noise. Instead, his shoulders heaved up and down like an impression of Tommy Cooper. I shot him a dirty look and widened my eyes in desperation. Minos wasn't for letting go of my hand and gripped it tighter when I tried to wriggle free. Then he started saying 'married lady, no problem here. Minos your friend'. We continued along, with Minos pulling me along the narrow path towards the Roman rock cut cisterns. So large, you can walk inside them, cut deep into the hard rock, in square cave like fashion; they are supported by a series of huge stone columns to support the roof. Regularly used to collect fresh rainwater from the mountains above, when the Acropolis was a busy thriving city.

Minos reluctantly let go of my hand, as I ventured to walk into one of the three cisterns originally built. We had brought a couple of strong light torches, and shining them to the very back of the cistern, we couldn't see over to the other side.

This was as far as Minos' went as travel guide, and we insisted that he walked back to the car park by himself, as we wanted to carry on walking down to the bottom of the gorge. Invading my personal space, and with his pungent smell of goats, he said, Patrizia, you kiss George. So I did!—THEN! He said, 'now kiss Minos'!! A slap in the face with a wet kipper would have been more welcome than obeying his request!! Backing away from him, and both hands up in defense, I said, 'Oh! No Minos, I cannot do that' and started walking away. Turning to Chris he smiled and showing his brown stained teeth again looked expectantly as Chris handed him a five euro note for his trouble, telling him to go and get himself a drink at the taverna in the village.

Thanking us both, he waved and smiled to return to the taverna and asked if we would be joining him later on after our walk. Half nodding and smiling, we just said, 'Maybe'. Off he went, and we both stood still, watching him climb quickly up the goat track path until he was out of sight!

We both sat down on a rock near the cisterns and laughed so much, tears ran down our face at a most bizarre and unusual afternoon at Eleftherna!!

CHAPTER 8
ASOMATI SCHOOL, PSILORITIS MOUNTAINS

'What shall we do today? I asked Chris, looking out the window on a grey morning in November.

'I thought we could drive in the Psiloritis mountains and have Sunday lunch at the lovely taverna/restaurant in Asomati village, came the reply.

Setting off at 11-30 a.m. for a one and half hours drive, through winding roads and breathtaking countryside, we eventually arrive at our favourite place to eat.

This remote and pretty village nestling high in the Psiloritis mountains where time has stood still, has the Greek generosity and old fashioned charm of a typically traditional Greek taverna. It is so small, you could pass by and not notice it was there. We discovered it quite by accident last year when we were doing one of our 'scouting days' and looking or new places to visit and do some walking. A large ruined Monastery set amongst mature palm trees and lush grass is situated at an angle to the village square.

It was raining very hard as we came to a halt on the car park outside the gates of the ruined Monastery, and making a sudden dash for it, we quickly opened the door of the taverna. Met by the heat coming from the centrally situated wood burning stove in the room, we took our seats near the kitchen which had several large pans bubbling away on top of the stove.

'They have BBQ'd spit roasted lamb on the menu, Chris said, I fancy having some of that today'. Looking round us, a few tables were already occupied with groups of local men sitting together in conversation and eating their Sunday lunch.

Vasili's Mother came over to us, and smiling, she asked us what we would like to drink. A few minutes later after she had brought our refreshments, some of her lovely home made red wine. Vasili, her son, came to us, and I asked him what was on the menu today. He motioned for us to come and take a look in the kitchen. Tina, Vasili's wife was busy serving a customer, and greeted us as we entered. Promptly lifting each lid of the pans on the stove, he told us there was boiled rice, boiled and roast potatoes, with horta, (wild greens collected from the mountain side). Opening the oven door, he said, that the BBQ'd lamb from his Fathers farm and the roasted chickens.

Chris was adamant he wanted to try the BBQ'd roast lamb, whilst I decided to have the home roast chicken; both with boiled and roast potatoes and horta. As my back was turned towards the other locals while we ate, I didn't notice straight away some of the colourful characters in the room. A serious debate was in progress regarding world affairs, as they watched the news on the television in the corner.

Introductions were made as we ordered a karafe of wine to compliment the meal. Tina told us in excellent English, she worked in Rethymnon at a book shop and helped out each Sunday at the family restaurant. Returning to the kitchen to continue cooking, she left us to enjoy our delicious meal in peace. I watched Chris munch his way through the heaped plate of food, and ended with chewing on the remains of his lamb bones held between his fingers, grinning at me in pure contentment. We had more or less finished all the food which was offered to us and sat back on our chairs as another karafe of wine was brought by Vasili's mum, Constantina.

Vasili had already told us that Constantina cooked everything, and even made the bread you have there; as well as making her own wine! He proudly said as he started clearing the dishes away. 'Nosteemo' I said in a loud voice, (delicious!) as Chris poured us another wine. I had turned my chair round again so I faced into the room, to watch the continuously animated conversations between the local guys.

By now, both Tina and Vasili had eaten their midday meal on the table near us, and Constantina continued to serve an ever growing number of people coming in to eat. I told Tina I was writing a book about travelling to Crete in our motorhome, and she asked me what the title would be, so she could keep a look out for it when it was published. I haven't decided yet, I replied, but I will let you know as soon as I do.

Sitting with for a while, she asked about our lives in England and our family. We in turn, asked her about the local mountain people, their way of life and traditions. Tina related our conversation to her Mother-in-law who was stood nearby listening and smiling. I told Tina to tell her that we had thoroughly enjoyed the meal, and this was our favourite place to eat. In rapid Greek, she rattled off our conversation, and in response, Constantina put her hand over her heart, and inclining her head, said Afgharisto.

The old guy sitting next to me, could speak and understand English as with a light tap on my arm, asked where we were from. I replied, we are from the North West of England. He told me that he had worked in England in 1979, in a place called Liverpool, do you know it?

Yes, I do, we are not that far away from Liverpool, only a few kilometers away infact.

I like it there, it was a good place, and I found a Greek taverna to go and eat and sit with other Greek men.

He continued asking me about the English economy, and comparing it with the Greek economy, saying that the average hourly wage in Greece is just three euro's an hour.

A few minutes later, we literally got bombarded with pertinent questions from the other guys sat at the tables nearby. A young man asked me through our interpreter, about English pensions. By then, I had recruited Chris in to help me out in the finer details of our pension schemes. He later told Chris that his brother worked in Scotland as a doctor.

An elderly jolly faced man asked me quite pointedly if I was a Christian! Ofcourse, came my reply. 'Do you worship the Virgin Mary, he said and pointed to a very beautiful iconic picture of the Virgin Mary and Jesus in her arms. Oxi (No) I said, but we love and respect her all the same.

Again—Oxi—Church of England, I said determinedly.

Then he proceeded to go into the details of how they cross themselves, and asked me if I did, and how I did it. I felt I was getting out of my depth, AGAIN!! And turned round to Chris for help; only to be met by the familiar look I got when I was accosted by Minos.

'You have done it again, he said quietly, got yourself into one of those tricky situations'. So I looked at my interpreter for help, who must have seen the desperate look on my face, and spoke a few sentences of rapid Greek to the old guy to quickly silence him. Vasili told us that he had drawn and painted the picture of Madonna and child which hung on the wall behind me. We were very impressed and said that he should do some more pictures and hang them on the walls for the summer visitors to purchase.

Turning away, I started to watch the busy little family as they continued their working day. Contented in their simplistic lifestyle at the restaurant, amongst the local people from the village who know and love them. To farm their delicious food and drink their home made wine, surrounded by the never ending beauty of the Psiloritis mountains, surely this was utopia?

Before leaving to head back down the mountains before dark, I asked them if I could take a photograph for my book, as I intended writing about this lovely place. They were all very pleased and flattered and we said that we would come back here for our Sunday lunch the following week before driving back to England.

'Do you think you will have a BBQ'd sheeps head next week, Vasili? Chris asked.

'I think I have one left today, you can take with you, he replied.

A few minutes later, Vasili returned with the cooked sheeps head in a large carrier bag, along with a decanted bottle of his mums delicious red wine. 'These are for you, a present from us here at the

Shaking our heads in wonder at their generosity and genuine affection, we hugged, kissed and shook hands to say goodbye for another week, and looked forward to seeing our little family from the mountains in Crete.

CHAPTER 9
CRETE TO ENGLAND

The heavy, continuous rains came January and February, forcing us to re-think our outdoor pursuits. Comfortable, cosy and warm, we enjoyed our little villa through the winter months. Reading a novel or writing my book, playing board games, whilst the constant heavy rain battered the plants and trees around the pool.

Walking in the little towns and villages, or collecting driftwood from the beach when the rain stopped for a while and the watery sun showed its face again. We enjoyed this relaxed, laid back way of life; but too soon, it was time to make plans and drive back to England.

Our intention was to catch the ferry from Suda Bay, Chania again, over to the Greek mainland; then an onward journey to Venice. Sometimes it is difficult to get plans just right on pre-booked ferry trips, as we will occasionally have the urge to be spontaneous and do a bit of sightseeing along the way at a familiar sounding town or City. This was one of those incidents as Chris had not only booked our trip from Crete to mainland Piraeus, but our onward trip to Venice from the port at Patras further down the coast!

The final day came for us to leave behind our little villa for a while. Cleaning and covering all the furniture until next time was completed, but as we locked the doors and shutters, my eyes filled with tears! I felt I was ready to go back to England and see family and friends, but we were leaving good friends here too!

My husband saw I was upset, and pulling me close to him said, 'We'll be back soon, Patti, don't cry'. That made me worse, and I curled into him and sobbed for a few minutes.

We sat quietly in our motor home on the National Road, watching a constant stream of traffic whizz by us on their way towards Chania. We were due out at 9-00 p.m. for Piraeus, on an overnight sailing, arriving early next morning. Chris told me that the onward ferry, The Lefka Ori, to Venice would be leaving two days later at midnight for a thirty six hour sailing, giving us two nights on board.

'We drive past the ancient City of Korinthos, I said, its on the way to Patras'. I was gazing intently at our map book sitting in the cabin, after we had boarded the ferry bound for the port of Piraeus. 'There is a lot of Roman archaeology there, and it would be an interesting diversion to find a campsite nearby and stay for a while'

Next morning, we were disappointed to wake early to the sound of pouring rain and dark skies. We resigned ourselves to a typically 'English weather Day', as we drove away from the boat and exited the gates of the port. Driving away from Athens, we followed the coastal road towards Korinthos. I watched the windscreen wipers beat a fast and regular rhythm, as I stared out at the cold dark morning. Eventually, we turned towards Korinthos and parked on an almost deserted stretch of land to watch the turbulent waves, as they crashed onto the beach, heavily littered with washed up flotsam and jetsam.

'What now' I said, pulling my face at Chris, as he stared out towards the rough sea.

'We are going to get really soaked going out in this weather'.

'It might ease off later today, Chris replied optimistically. 'We'll put our waterproofs and walking boots on, and go into the town for something to eat and do a bit of shopping'.

The modern town of Korinthos is really nice, and we enjoyed wandering round the shops despite the rain. However, the heavy rain was relentless, so eventually, we took refuge in a café for a late lunch. As we watched the leaking roof drip constantly with the heavy deluge of rain, buckets were strategically placed under the holes in the roof; and soon filled up several containers of rain water! We had dashed into the café, and slowly peeled our wet layers off, laughing at the rain water dripping from our hair and down our faces; suspended momentarily on the end of my nose! HA!!

Many local people were rushing home to their warm houses, as we shrugged our wet coats on again, once we had had our meal. The bad weather had set in for the day, and it appeared to be going dark at just three o clock in the afternoon. A sodden leaflet had been placed under our windscreen wipers as we returned to the motor home. Stretching forward, I took it inside with me, and after struggling out of our wet clothes I carefully opened the leaflet so it didn't tear. It was an advertising leaflet regarding a new campsite which had opened in the summer, stating that it was in walking distance from ancient Korinthos. Reading it out to Chris, he replied, 'why not ring them then?

Tapping the number into my mobile phone, I heard a friendly male voice at the other end of the phone. Asking him where the site actually was, I explained that we had got his number from a leaflet placed under the windscreen wipers on our motor home. He started to tell me the directions from the marina car park to his campsite, and also asked me if I knew Korinthos at all. I replied, that we were strangers here, and didn't know the area at all. Pausing for a moment, he announced that he would come to collect us in his car, and escort our motorhome back to the site!

Amazing!! I cut our connection and related the conversation to Chris. A few minutes later, a saloon car drove towards us from the main road, with an elderly gentleman and a young woman of about 25 years old. Speaking fluent English, she introduced herself and her grandfather, and asked us to follow them to the site.

It took fifteen minutes to leave the modern town behind and wind through several smaller roads before reaching the pretty campsite on the outskirts of the town. The rain was still steadily coming down as we both got a fresh dousing to park, and connect the van up to their electricity supply.

Whether the nice old grandfather felt sorry for us, or he was just behaving with the natural Greek generosity, we don't know for sure! After half an hour, an urgent knock came on the door of our van, as Chris opened it, we saw the nice old man smiling up at us with a tray containing two cups of hot chocolate and a plate of toast in one hand, and in the other hand, a large umbrella to shelter him from the heavy rain. 'For you! He said solemnly, before walking back to the farmhouse.

'Did you ask him for some food when you went over to see him about the 'hook up' earlier? I said, looking astonished.

No! I didn't mention food at all, Chris replied.

We were both cold and hungry, and devoured his kind offerings graciously.

The rain continued for the rest of the day and into the evening, so we resigned ourselves to staying put for the rest of the day, and having our evening meal in the motor home. About ten minutes into peeling some potatoes, a gentle knock came on the door of the van. We both looked at each other in surprise, as Chris opened the door to reveal our 'evening take-a-way meal' brought to us by our congenial host.

'Oh! How lovely, I said, standing behind Chris and thanking him.

As Chris took the current tray of food from him, I passed him the previous tray with the clean cups and plates.

'Efaristo poli' (thank you very much) I enthused, as he waved to us again, and walked back to the farmhouse.

'What has he brought us this time,' I said, lifting the cover. 'It looks like home made Mousakka'. As I set the table, Chris poured some chilled wine from the fridge, and we sat down to enjoy our delicious, but unexpected meal.

We both heard the heavy rain on and off through the night, drumming constantly on the roof of our motor home. So we were relieved next morning to look out and see that it had finally stopped. Fortunately, Chris was already washed and dressed when another light tapping came on the door of our van! I dived under the duvet as Chris opened the door once more. A few minutes went by as I heard muffled voices coming from Chris and the old gentleman. Finally, he said 'you can come out now, he's gone, and he has brought our Sunday morning breakfast!

Oh! It's too kind of him, I exclaimed, jumping out of bed to inspect the tray. 'I wonder if he treats all the campers like this, or we just look hungry and need a good meal.

'No idea, Chris replied munching the latest offering, just eat your breakfast and enjoy it'.

Returning the tray with clean cups and plates, we asked our kind benefactor for directions to the archaeological site of Korinthos. Walking through the sleepy village near the campsite, we eventually come to the beginning of attractive block paved roads leading up, in a gradual incline to the elevated ruins of the city. It reminded us of the magnificent Acropolis in Athens, but on a much smaller scale. The original site goes back to Neolithic times, and over centuries, it has been destroyed and rebuilt from many invaders to become an important Roman city. Continuing excavations are still being carried out as it is on many other prestigious sites.

Entering through the gates to a pay booth, we were immediately joined by a large friendly dog. Wagging his tail constantly, he licked my hand and looked lovingly up as we moved along to start our tour of the site. Our four legged friend quite happily escorted us round the ruins, and leading the way, he would periodically stop at each point of interest to sniff round and then look back at us as if to say 'come and look at this, you will find this interesting'. He was quite comical in his antics, and made us laugh with delight to be escorted in such a different manner.

A very important city in its day, the ornate stone structures had been carefully and painstakingly restored to their original beauty, giving the enthusiastic amateur a taste of how things would have been. From their humble homes, to a row of shops, leading up to the exquisite bathhouses and theatres; we eventually come to admire the senate building, where scribes and elders would have made decisions and wrote laws to govern the city. We walked where the noble citizens walked, and due to an immense amount of ancient debris, initially dug out by large machinery and dumped to make a pathway; we were literally walking on large amounts of impacted Roman pottery.

Wandering around for nearly two hours, we eventually arrived back at our starting point. By then, our four legged friend had found someone new to re-start his tour! Before we left, I asked the lady at the pay booth about the dog. She said he belonged to the site, and he earns his keep by escorting tourists around the ruins of Korinthos!

Next morning, we started packing up and stowing our things away to move on towards the ferry at Patras for an early evening sailing. Chris walked across to the farmhouse after breakfast to tell 'Georgie' our nice old man that we were leaving around lunchtime for the ferry and could we settle the bill. Whilst I busied myself with washing up, I looked out of the window and saw the two of them in animated conversation. Georgie grasped Chris with one hand, then pulling him towards his chest in a bear hug; gave him a friendly smack of his back with the other hand.

AHhh!! Friends forever there, I thought, as I watched them slowly walk towards the motor home and stop outside. Opening the door, I greeted Georgie and thanked him for our lovely stay on the site. Smiling back at me, he said he hoped that we would pass this way again next year and come to stay with them.

'You have found a new friend there', I said to Chris after he had shut the door again.
'Yes! I think I have, Chris replied. I asked him if I could settle the bill for two nights stay, plus the food he so very kindly brought us, and he said it would be ten euro's'.
'What!! I replied.
'Ten euro's' Chris repeated, so I gave him fifteen euro's and told him to buy a drink for himself'.
Still in conversation regarding Georgie's generosity, the familiar tap came on the door! This time, I opened it to see our smiling host with a big bag of oranges from his orchard and a large bottle of homemade red wine held in each hand.
'For You' he repeated once again.

Being an emotional person, his kind gesture overwhelmed me, and climbing down the steps, I reached out to give him a big hug and kiss as I babbled away in English telling him kind he was, and very typical of the Greek people's generosity.

Leaving the campsite early afternoon towards our next destination, we finally said goodbye and a big thank you to a remarkable old man who had made our stay memorable. Joining the E65—the main road running alongside the sea, we cruised along at a steady pace enjoying the better weather and lovely scenery. It was Chris who first noticed the continuous line of Roman excavations facing out towards the sea. Extensive road works were still in the process of widening the E65 to help ease the volume of traffic. Unfortunately, there wasn't anywhere at all we could stop and take a closer look as we were on the opposite side of the road and couldn't do a u.turn.

It was going dark, as we pulled into the dock gates and started looking for a booking office for some information. As we were approaching the port, we both noticed a lot of young men in large groups either walking alongside the huge iron fencing surrounding the port, or actually inside the port grounds.

'Where have all these guys come from Chris? I said, as we drove past a small group of five men, having previously noticed us, were now following behind the van.

'I don't know, he replied, but the information desk is over there. I'll pull up and make some enquiries, wait here for me'.

By then, the group of five men had caught us up, and as Chris walked away they surrounded our motor home, looking under the van and peering at me through the window. I quickly reached forward to lock both doors and continued to watch them through the wing mirrors. One guy was looking intently at the ladder, at the back of the van, which goes up and onto the roof, whilst the others continued to bend low and look underneath.

Sheer panic rose in my throat and instead of screaming for help, I put my hand on the car horn and pressed it very hard, holding it down, until Chris came back and shooed them away.

'It's okay Patti, he said, as I let him in the van, they're gone now'. We re-parked the motor home, this time with the back end up to a solid structure, so as to deter anyone attempting to climb up the ladder. A few minutes later, some more youths came by the van, and started looking underneath and in through the windows. Chris half opened his window and told them to go away.

'Ah! You speak English, one cheeky guy said, and tried to get into friendly conversation with us. By now, I started to get really upset, as we had two hours to wait before boarding and I was frightened of what they might do to the motor home if they turned nasty.

'Let's move the van again, I said to Chris, as more young guys came to join in and look us over. We moved the motor home another three times before finding some port security men who directed us over to where a few lorries were parked ready for boarding. The security men told us the young men were trying to board the ferry illegally to get to Italy and other E.U countries. We watched one young man continually run up the gang plank leading into the interior car deck, only to be chased away by a diligent security man. We both agreed that if the guy managed to get on board, undetected, he wouldn't have much trouble in finding somewhere to hide!

As we took our turn in the queue to board, every vehicle was thoroughly searched inside and out. We both encouraged the security men to look inside our motor home and told them about the guys looking under the van, and up at the ladder which leads to the roof. They asked us if they could climb up and take a quick inspection, whilst another guy looked underneath with a torch. We told them we would be pleased if they did.

Our two nights and one day sailing to Venice was very relaxing, and our large cabin had twin beds instead of narrow bunk beds. As with all the other ferryboats, we were in comfortable surroundings with good food and entertainment en route. So it became a mini weekend holiday for us.

We arrived at the port of Venezia at 7-00 a.m. on a bright, but cold and frosty morning. Quickly disembarking, we drove out following the clearly marked exit signs towards the centre of Venice. We were soon driving over a large bridge, surrounded by calm seas. I spotted a car parking sign to our right and with careful negotiation; it brought us to a stop on a large car park with other caravans and motor homes parked up for the day. We walked back and out of the double gates towards a busy area with Japanese tourists alighting from some coaches.

'We'll follow them, Chris said in a low voice, they all seem to know where the water bus is'.

Walking through a small market with gift shops and souvenirs, we saw several people buying tickets for the water bus at a small booth. Doing likewise, we sat down on the bus waiting to be taken to St Marks Square, the very heart of Venice.

As we pulled away from the quayside, the lagoon opened up to reveal THE MOST mystical scenery with a few tiny fishing boats dotted on a millpond like sea. The low morning mist banked and swirled over the calm surface, along with an early morning sun rise, painting the sky with splashes of deep reds and orange. The surreal image reminded me of the muted colours in a painting by Monet. We held our breath and stared for a while to try and keep this beautiful image in our minds eye; rather like taking a lasting photograph when the shutter clicks. The sun rays shimmered on the surface of the misty lagoon casting a warm glowing 3D effect.

Tearing our eyes away from such amazing natural beauty, we turned our heads to look at the true magnificence of the Venetian harbor, and the perfect line of opulent buildings running alongside the promenade. Already busy with tourists, we left the water bus and walked into the old City. A large network of narrow canals had many brightly decorated gondolas already cruising along with honeymoon couples or small families. As they sat on the luxuriously padded seats, the young gondoliers with their familiar black trousers and striped jumpers, smiled as they punted under the little arched bridges.

We walked through the narrow alleyways, remarking on the high sided buildings, built to give maximum shade from the long hot summers. Pretty restaurants and cafes were dotted along the walkways and feeling hungry and thirsty we chose a charming little café for our morning brunch. Entering a little doorway, we were greeted by the waitress who pointedly asked us what nationality we were, as she could speak five languages and wished to communicate in our native tongue. Surprised and impressed, we sat down and ordered our meal.

Our day trip coincided with a special concert of Mozart's music throughout the week. As we wandered through the city, many young actors dressed in period theatre costumes were handing leaflets out to tourists which advertised forthcoming recitals. As there are so many beautiful old churches in Venice, a few are being used as venues for various concerts. We walked into one church, the familiar strains of Mozart echoing around its ancient walls. Sitting for a while to listen and contemplate, we glanced round the rich opulent interior with intricately dark wood carvings.

We had a lot of fun looking round the clusters of beautifully decorated shops which sold many different kinds of Venetian masks for the ever popular masquerade ball. Every theme, colour, style and design you could imagine. Large and small, there was something to suit everyone's taste. Chris bought me a pretty autumn coloured one, which has pride of place on my bedroom wall.

Hand in hand, we stroll back to where some gondolas were berthed, and asking me if I would like a punt down the canals to see Venice by boat; we sit down in a rather gaudy red and gold one. Expecting the gondolier to break into a rendition of a well known Italian piece of music, he gently punts down the quiet canals alongside the slowly sinking Venetian buildings. We certainly had a different perspective of Venice as we slowly cruised along under the many little arched bridges and past the narrow walkways running alongside the canals.

Wishing that we could have had more time in Venice, and agreeing to come back again one day for much longer, we made our way back to the water bus and returned to the car park and our motor home.

Plotting an alternative route from the one we had taken on the way to Crete, we intended missing out much of Germany and Switzerland, as our family had told us previously, they were going up to the mountains for a skiing holiday. Heading north westerly through Italy, towards the city of Turino, well known for the famous 'Shroud of Turin'. We wild camped for two or three nights on quiet lay by, well away from the busy autobahn. Our main purpose each day was to make sure we had enough fresh water, and to keep our cassette toilet clean and empty. We just about managed to do both, and on the fourth day, we drove into the lovely city of Turino to park up near the broad river, framed by mature trees running parallel to the city.

We didn't have much chance of getting to see the 'Turin Shroud' which is kept in the royal chapel of the Cathedral of St. John the

Baptist, so in consolation, we had some Italian ice cream as we strolled along the banks of the river in the winter sunshine.

It was nearing the end of February, as we continued to drive north; the air becoming much colder and fresher. Out came more thick wooly jumpers to keep us from shivering in the morning air. Our motor home was warm and comfortable when we were on the move, and when we stopped to park up for the night; we would use the Calor gas heating system. It was during the night when temperatures dropped further, the van would be freezing first thing in the morning when we got up to put the kettle on for a wash and a coffee.

BRrrr! Then, it was so cold, you could see your breath inside the van!

One particularly cold morning, I was scrambling around the bed on my hands and knees under the duvet looking for some extra clothing I had worn to bed and discarded during the night. Frustrated, not being able to find them, I was moaning and mumbling until I heard Chris laughing at me.

'You look like a tortoise under the duvet, WHAT ARE you doing??

'Looking for my clothes came the curt reply, and I am NOT coming out until I find some—I'm freezing!! More laughter!!!!

We were heading for the St Bernard's tunnel in the Alps. As we approached, the magnificent mountain range covered in snow came into view. Joining the queue to pay our thirty euro's at one of the booths, we were waved through to continue our journey. All the roads were clear of snow, but remained wet and icy in parts, caution notices were in place as we drove at a steady pace along the many twists and turns in the road. Continuous snow had fallen along the mountain range which was thickly covered in glistening white snow, reflecting back from the bright sunny day.

'The snow looks much finer and powdery almost, so high up, I said looking across to the base of the mountains. 'Almost like icing sugar on a huge Christmas cake.

Chris nodded in agreement and said he was pleased that the roads were so clear, as he wasn't sure if we would be able to get through with our motor home without any problems.

Sometime later, we reached the pretty town of Besancon, in France. I persuaded Chris to stop at a lovely little hotel and book us in for one night bed and breakfast. What I really needed was a good hot shower and a warm room for one night's luxury after 'wild camping' for a few nights. Rushing into the bathroom the moment we got our key, I squealed with delight as I saw a large bath just waiting to be filled to the brim with hot soapy bubbles!! And for me to sink thankfully down and have them right up to my chin!!

Both scrubbed clean and fresh, we sauntered down to the dining room and had the most delicious meal with an obligatory bottle of chilled French wine. It was a lovely evening and well worth the extra expense on our journey back to England.

Arriving at the port of Rotterdam, we boarded the boat early evening for another overnight sailing, arriving the next morning to a very cold and gloomy wet day. A security search inside and out of our motor home by three pleasant security staff, and in friendly conversation, asked us where we had been. Totally amazed by our answer, we told them briefly of our many adventures and that we hoped to be able to fly out in five months time to stay for a few months in our villa in Crete.

'You must be feeling very cold at present, we have had a terrible winter here in England' one security man said, as Chris told them of my doing a good impression of a tortoise under the duvet one cold morning.

We were on the homeward stretch now, and Chris remarked that he had to really concentrate on driving on the left hand side of the road, especially coming up to roundabouts. We actually didn't have a home to go back to, as our house was still occupied at that time. But over the following five months, we not only got our house back, but decorated it throughout, and did the gardens. Once we were settled, we started making plans for our four month holiday in the villa, starting in August 2011.

Returning to the beloved island of Crete, we have many more exciting adventures, meet lots more interesting and colourful characters. Discover new places to see and find previously unknown gorges to do our walks.

Join us, as we venture into some remote, far flung mountain villages and together, we discover, THE TRUE SPIRIT OF CRETE!!

CHAPTER 10
MELIDONI CAVE & DHISKORI MONASTRY

AUGUST 2011

It had been raining constantly with heavy thunderstorms lasting four days. When it finally stopped, we took our map from the bookshelf to see where we could visit for the day.

As we drove along the National Road towards the holiday resort of Panormo, the day was fine and sunny, but with a few black clouds threatening more rain. Following the tourist signs for Melidoni Cave, we started climbing steadily up towards the Kouloukonas mountain range some 1075m and pausing at the side of the road, we looked across at the amazing low cloud formation, lazily drifting down, and curling across the mountain peaks so it looked like there was smoke coming out of the tops.

Arriving at Melidoni Cave sometime later, we walked towards the entrance and bought our tickets, and an information booklet telling us of the long and varied history of the cave. There has been a settlement there as far back as the 14th century, mentioned in documents by the Venetians. The information pays particular attention to the martyrs in 1824, where 370 civilians and 30 soldiers fleeing from the Turks were put to death inside the cave. Ten years later, a man called Pashley dug into the cave and found the tragic remains of the dead. It is said that he was actually treading on the bones and skulls of these poor people as he entered. An impressive stone memorial known as Room of the Heroes holds centre stage as you enter the cave from above.

Carefully picking our way down the incline with uneven stone steps, slippery by constant dripping water from above. We gazed at the large interior through dimly lit spot lights which highlighted some magnificently large stalagmites. Never having seen so many stalagmites and stalactites situated in one place before, some far thicker than a man's thigh; hanging from way up at the top of the cave, or thrusting upwards in various ornate designs some twenty or thirty feet high.

Standing at the very bottom of the cave, we let our eyes follow the varying amounts of stalagmites; some were flat like mushrooms stacked on top of each other. The interior gave the impression of a huge cathedral with massive organ pipes, quite awe inspiring in fact in such stately manner.

There have been a large amount of archaeological finds over many years, dating from Neolithic, through to late Minoan and Roman artifacts. There is strong evidence that a phallus shaped stalagmite was used as a symbol of worship! The archaeologists have found a large number of small figurines of naked and dressed females dating to around the end of 7th century at the base of the stalagmite. This was presumed to have been a goddess who was worshipped there for a time.

We reluctantly came away and promised to go back in the future to take another look, as we were so impressed with the cave and its history; and would be thrilled to return once again.

Passing through the tiny hamlet of Agia (Saint) we remarked that they must have run out of Saints names, and just called the village Agia—until they could think one up!! Driving along, we noticed on both sides of the road, there were large amounts of cut tree trunks. Nearby, there are a few 10 foot cube shaped concrete buildings. From a hole in the top of the roof, continuous thick black smoke bellowed out. Slowing down to take a better look, we started noticing some vent holes at the side of the structures, which also emitted the black smoke. There were large amounts of fine black dust in the surrounding areas, and literally everything was covered with it.

Eventually, Chris said that he thought they were making charcoal, and the cube shaped buildings were charcoal ovens! Never seeing this process before, we guessed that the village of Agia, made their living at producing charcoal.

Driving along, we see a large pickup truck coming towards us on the road ahead. He was heavily laden down with recently cut olive branches, stacked very high at the back of his vehicle, and bulging out at each side. We see a lot of farmers this time of year, busily pruning their trees in the olive groves. They will either take the cut branches for their sheep and goats, or 'burn off'. The burning off process is permitted between October and April, where you will see continual plumes of smoke in the distance, or nearby, locals tending a large fire at the side of the road by their olive grove.

Pausing for a while to stretch our legs and to walk round the Traditional village of Mourtzana, built in the Venetian style, the large and somewhat derelict properties are to be found at the back of the small settlement from the road. As we walk between the olive groves along a dirt track, the sweetest little brown dog started wagging his tail from behind a wire fence. He looked as though he belonged to one of the local farmers, who had him there to guard his sheep when he was older. But for the moment, the little puppy just wanted to play! Calling him in a prolonged greeting, he runs towards us, then stops, then runs again, all the while his tail is wagging! Squeezing through the wire fence, he puts his front legs against mine and with his mouth slightly open; his little pink tongue hangs to one side as he invites me to tickle his ears and stroke his head!

'Oh! What a cute little dog, I said to Chris beaming down at my new friend. He loves all this attention, look at his tail wagging.

'Come on Patti, he will start to follow us and then get himself lost'.

'Time to go little dog, I said, giving him a final petting.

He tried to delay my decision by putting both his front paws on the top of my feet to delay our leaving.

As we walked away, back down the olive groves, I turned briefly to see my little dog still wagging his tail at us until we were out of sight. Spending a little time wandering through the narrow alleyways of a typically ruined Venetian village with heavy old wooden doors and shutters, bleached and rotting with many years of hot Greek sunshine, now hung at lopsided angles, abandoned and virtually forgotten. Ornate lintels above some of the doors had deeply carved patterns in the old stone work, still visible from Venetian time. A rusting old olive press was still in situ inside one of the derelict houses, with a thick olive wood beam wedged between the press and the ceiling.

Returning to the car, we are now heading for Dhiskouri Monastery, which Chris had read about in our travel guide book. It informed him that the Monastery had been abandoned around the Turkish invasion, and in 1995 a monk had moved back to live there and restore the place to its original condition. On the continuous climb roughly between Garazo and Axos villages high in the Psiloritis mountains, we eventually find the tiny Monastery set a little way back from the quiet road. Chris had actually driven past it before we saw the pretty whitewashed church further along which belongs to the Monastery.

Walking back downhill, we pass a very old water well with an attractive stone structure arching over to protect it, but also used as a shrine to Agios Georgiou's, which is the name of the Monastery as well. Continuing along, we pause to admire the monk's vegetable garden and the large amount of cut olive trees for his wood stove later in the year. An old stone water well is positioned nearby to help water his crops on a daily basis in the summer months.

'He seems to be very self sufficient, I remarked, as Chris gently knocked on the wooden door of the Monastery; to be allowed to enter by one of his helpers a young man who returned to the modern sounds of television coming from one of the buildings nearby.

The interior courtyard was of cobbled paving and with one or two large spruce trees, gave maximum shelter from hot sunshine. Towards the restored and comfortable living area, cloth covered wooden benches ran alongside the wall, with two sleeping cats, their bodies entwined around each other! A few home grown large gourds hang suspended from the elongated wooden terracing. At the far end of the courtyard beneath one of the mature trees, lie two horizontal stone tombs of previous Abbots. One Abbot was born in 1812 and died in 1920, making him 108 years old!!!

Returning to the little wooden porch on our entrance into the Monastery, I light a candle amongst the many beautiful old icons of Saints, and coming out into bright sunshine, notice by the side of the door is the loveliest icon of St George slaying the Dragon set in a niche in the wall. On closer inspection, with its rich colour glinting in the sunlight, we guessed the icon could be coloured marble or a semi precious stone.

Walking back, up the quiet road, we went to take a look in the tiny church of Ayios Yeoryios (St George). Passing several trees heavy with oranges, we walked up the narrow pathway to the door of the church. Turning the old circular handle I stooped to enter inside. Adjusting my eyes to the gloomy interior, I caught my breath as I gazed in wonder at the many beautiful religious artifacts laid out before me. We had both stepped in by now, and pushed the door shut as it was so small inside. It only took two steps up the central aisle to the altar, which was freshly hung with pretty lace curtaining normally put there for weddings or christenings. A large leather bible bound in gold coloured filigree and inset with five oval pictures of saints lay on the narrow alter table. Carefully opening the book, the pages were ornately written in red and black calligraphy, familiar in religious texts. A communion wine vessel was placed nearby and behind the old bible an intricately carved metal cross was standing. Even the monks white cassock and surplus was hanging behind the curtained area. Heavily embroidered cloths covered the alter and a small low table, near some stacked wooden chairs for the congregation. Large brass candlesticks adorned the alter, placed each side of the heavy bible.

'How can this be, I said shaking my head totally mystified, how can anyone leave all these lovely old things here and the door unlocked?

'I don't know, Chris replied, they seem to be very trusting here in the mountains, but how can anyone stoop so low as to steal from a church; they wouldn't give that a second thought?

We journeyed along on our circular trip to a village called Livadhia, a typical mountain village, self sufficient and very busy with local people going about their business when we arrived. Squeezing into a parking place on the narrow road, with a steep slope from the fragmented concrete road completely broken away, I carefully wriggled out of the car and edged past the crumbling road on tip toes. Our stomachs were rumbling as we chose a busy restaurant to order the best giros we have ever tasted. The filling is locally cooked lamb or goat, with fresh salad and chips, nestling on a bed of Greek yoghurt and placed inside soft warm pita bread, YUM!!

Looking round at the many local guys who had recently come in after a hard day's work, to have a drink and some conversation. There were two men dressed in shabby work clothes, hands rough and calloused from manual work. They looked like identical twins, as they sat 'mirror imaging' each other. Thick, black curly hair and an overgrown beard and mustache framed their dark swarthy faces, lined and weathered from years of working outside in harsh weather. A very over weight guy sat near them, his back to the wall with one eye on the television in the corner, the other one scanning round periodically to listen to various conversations. Catching my eye once or twice, he smiled and raising his drink, said 'yammas' to us, to which we returned the greeting.

Our meal was delicious and plenty of it, and as I ate it hungrily remarked to Chris whether it was sheep or goat meat. He said he didn't know, but wouldn't be surprised if it was goat meat, as it seems to be in abundance up in the mountains.

The sun was sinking slowly as we drove back down the mountain roads before it went dark.

Another very enjoyable day with lots of surprises and adventures.

CHAPTER 11
ANCIENT CITY OF GORTY'S—ALSO KNOWN AS GORTYNA

AUGUST 2011

The ancient city of Gorty's caught our eye one evening as we were both browsing through one of our books, regarding the archaeology of Crete.

Because Gorty's was in a southerly direction of the island, it would take a bit of forward planning and preparation to get there. We will have to drive for a few hours, Chris said that night. With prior knowledge to the roads on Crete, one minute they are quite smooth and passable, only to change quite dramatically the next with pothole roads and very uneven surfaces. Not at all passable, only with a four wheel drive or a willing donkey!!

Bearing this in mind, we rose very early next day and after thorough preparation the previous evening, set off for our journey to Gortyna.

The large ruined city of Gorty's is situated in the southern part of the island, so we would be passing through the towns of Armeni, Spili, Timbaki and Mires before reaching our destination.

As the majority of our journey encompassed the main highway with no hold ups, we made excellent progress. It is not unusual to see a small herd of goats grazing or walking down the centre of the road, or have to wait for a local farmer to bring his sheep and goats down the main road towards his farm buildings. But today, we were goat and sheep free!!

Turning away from the coast road a short distance from our villa and about 10km from the busy town of Rethymnon, we pass by the little village of Armeni, well known for the interesting Minoan cemetery, which can be visited throughout the year. It has over 200 tombs cut into the rock dating from the late Minoan period, after the fall of the great palaces. Situated beneath a large oak wood, the tombs are constructed as either chamber or passage burials, some have been left incomplete. There are several chambers which appear to be more impressive than the majority which could denote a person of rank or importance. As with any ancient site, the archaeological digs have revealed precious artifacts, jewellery and vases which have been placed in the museums at Rethymnon and Heraklion. As with any good mystery stories, they have yet to find the town from where these burials came and so the work continues.

Heading towards the beautiful town of Spili, the main road bypasses it! If you chose to drive by, you will miss this pretty place. The many narrow alleyways and white washed houses are carelessly arranged along the somewhat cobbled lanes. Ancient archways lead you through narrow streets with colourful Cretan flowers growing vigorously over ornate balconies, or in rusty olive oil tins clustered together against the walls. It is a busy working town with many shops and offices, farming and light industry. Large amounts of tourists arrive daily by bus or car and spend their day strolling around or having a delicious meal in one of the delightful restaurants in the square. It is a typical Grecian village, still holding onto the old customs and traditions.

Further along the main highway, the magnificent Oros Kedros Mountains rise up to 1,776 metres at their highest point. Low cloud surrounds the very top, swirling and breaking like giant pieces of cotton wool, giving a surreal image as we drive on toward Gorty's.

Approaching the industrial town of Timbaki, where their main industry appears to be growing bananas. We noticed the large numbers of polytunnels side by side over a vast area as we were on the outskirts of the town. There didn't appear to be much interest here, although one or two kafenions and restaurants had tried to make their premises look nice to attract visitors and encourage trade. One of our friends described the town as a hot dust bowl with very little interest to encourage one to stop and take a look, however, on our return journey, we did!

Between Timbaki and the small farming town of Mires, we quickly noticed that there had recently been extensive fires along the four kilometer route. No sign of life, human or animal, it had a very eerie feel to the charred and blackened scrub on both sides of the road.

Large raging fires had caused the bleak outlines of the olive trees, the remains of branches stuck out like blackened fingers against the contrasting blue sky. Where once there had been thorny shrubs for the local goat population to feed on, was now a hopeless barren landmass. It would take a couple of years or more to recover and rejuvenate itself. Temporary relief came in the form of a small concrete goat shelter or from some farm storage buildings, still standing from the massive raging fires recently.

Looking round us as we drove through the town of Mires I said, 'No tourism here either? Just some light industry and farming'. It was late morning and the sun climbed higher in the sky as we were both eager to see the well documented archaeology of ancient Gorty's it being one of the most important discoveries on Crete.

'Here it is' I said, looking at the parked cars at the side of the road, where a few curious tourists had pulled over to read the large information board. We parked at the back of the site, positioning the car under the shade of a large tree to help keep it cool. We bought our tickets and entered the site.

'It's a lot bigger than I thought it would be, I remarked, 'it seems to stretch over to the other side of the road as well, amongst the olive groves'.

Chris replied, that he had read that the City was so large; we would not see it all in one day!

The first part we saw seemed to be fully excavated; each building was carefully documented and labeled so the reader would know a brief history. From around Minoan times, the City rose to power under the Dorian's, probably not being invaded by them, but gradually settling there in peaceful order and in large numbers. By the eighth century BC, it had significant commercial power. The Dorian empire appeared to have a 'class system' with dominance over the Minoan surfs and slaves. Even for the ordinary citizens, life was hard at that time.

We were both overwhelmed at the carefully reconstructed site, and could see how the City must have looked when it was a busy metropolis. We were looking at the remains of the Town Hall or 'Odeion'. Reading the precise information it spoke of the heavy horizontal stone tablets, approximately nine metres long and three metres high at the front of the building. It was a proclamation of their law codes. Written from left to right and from right to left, in a continuous line, so that there were no breaks in the writing; it filled the whole of the front walls. After 67BC St Paul along with St Titus arrived in the City to preach Christianity to the people. The partially ruined church of St Titus, which was built around the sixth century, can still be seen behind a protective fence.

The City was eventually 'sacked' by the invading Saracens in the 9th century and Gorty's was left crumbling and abandoned!

We spent a lot of time wandering round this ancient city, and because there was still a lot of structure in place, coupled with extensive restoration, it didn't take much imagination to recall what it would have looked like when the Minoans and Dorian's lived there.

Eventually, we decided to walk over to the other side of the road and wander down the permitted path through the olive groves. Almost immediately, there was clear evidence of an early settlement with partially ruined buildings. A continuance of excavation work was still apparent as we walked round following a tall fenced off area. Through part of the open fencing, we gazed in awe at a lovely tiled mosaic floor, but a large part of it had fine sand over the top to protect from extreme elements here. Broken jars and cooking vessels, stone pillars intricately carved were all carefully labeled and piled to one side of the site, to be restored later.

Glancing down briefly to watch where I walked, I was flabbergasted to find I was actually walking on several pieces of broken pottery and other ancient relics on the rough stony path. They must have used a large digger to remove the top layers of soil and stone to initially uncover the site.

Retracing our steps to the road and the large information board we had spotted earlier. We both started reading about the 1800 year old olive tree nearby. It had literally grown round some marble pillars from the ruined site, its deep roots embedded around the pillars themselves!

'Have you read the bit about Ayii Dheka (St Ten, or the 10 Martyrs) Chris said, it's only a short distance down the road by foot'.

We decided to take a look whilst we were here. It takes its name from ten early Christians who were martyred here in 250 AD by the Roman Emperor Decius. The Holy Ten, are much admired and respected here in Crete, as they were the forerunners of early Christianity. To lay down their lives and oppose tyrannical opposition!

As we entered the tiny well kept, white washed church, our eyes were immediately drawn to the beautiful fresco depicting the ten martyrs. Looking at each one by one, they all appeared roughly about the same age, all except for one man who looked to have been in his twenties when he was executed by beheading. Very macabre, beneath the fresco and preserved under glass, the original stone block which was used in their decapitation can still be seen!!

It was time to leave. Deep in thought, we climbed back into the car for our long journey home. Presently, we spoke of our adventures of the day, and what we had seen—unbelievable, stunning, amazing were some of the words coming from our lips. Vowing to return again at some later date, to see and recall some of the many wonders of the ancient city of Gortyna.

CHAPTER 12
SPINALONGA ISLAND

AUGUST 2011

Having previously read the book The Island, we were both very keen to visit. Plans were made to drive to the pretty seaside town of Elounda and stay in accommodation over night, to include a short boat trip over to Spinalonga that day.

Setting off very early that morning, whilst the air was still quite cool; we climbed into the car at 7-30 a.m. Turning onto the National Road towards Heraklion in a north easterly direction, we remarked how quiet the roads were at this time of morning.

Our little car bobbed along over the sometimes rough patches in the road, with an occasional pot hole! As we passed alongside the lovely stretch of sandy beaches and coves we saw some early morning holiday makers out and about, with a few people already in the warm sea having a swim or merely relaxing and lying lazily around on their floats

Turning away from the gradual build up of traffic towards Heraklion, we followed the road signs towards Elounda. A few minutes later we were away from the busy industrial parts of Heraklion, and into the village of Malia which appears to attract the 18-25 year old generation, their current pastime being quad bikes! There must have been a dozen or more young people, sometimes two on one bike, riding down the centre of the main highway, impervious to other cars trying to get through. With the absence of safety helmets and wearing t-shirts and shorts, we slowed the car down to almost a crawl until we were clear of the village.

Descending gradually towards Elounda, we parked on the little marina facing the sea just before lunchtime, and remarked on the many visitors milling around the ticket booth for the ferry across to Spinalonga which ran every half hour in the summer months.

Reading the notice board of the crossing times, we realized we had just missed one and would have to wait a further twenty minutes before we could go across.

'Let's have a walk round the promenade at the restaurants along the bay, to chose a nice place to eat tonight, Chris said.

There were so many to choose from, and all with a nautical theme brightly decorated, with colourful tablecloths and flowers. Potted palms and plants framed the decked areas, some with a canopy of trailing vines or sweet smelling plants overhead.

Taking our place in the queue, we were helped on board by a crew member, to take our seats. Many other small boats were cruising past us as we sped towards the island, the warm wind in our hair and the sun beating down on the back of our necks. Slowing down as we were nearing the island, we eventually came to an abrupt stop as the ferry boat bumped along the side of the wooden landing stage.

As we alighted, we stood for a moment to look back over to Elounda village, with a lovely vista of shops and restaurants dotted along the shoreline. Our eyes travelled along and up to the ruined archway which led to the gated entrance of Spinalonga!

Built by the Venetians in 16th century, they named the walled City 'Olous'. Originally designed and built as a defensive fortress to protect Crete. Starting the building project in 1579 to approximately 1586, where repairs and re-structures were carried out during the Cretan War. At this time, rebels took sanctuary and continued to harass the Turks. Eventually, the Venetians withdrew after a long and bloody battle with the Turks. Around 1715 Muslims settled in the fortification to re-construct shops and houses on top of the ruined Venetian City. They prospered greatly and their population grew to around 200 local city dwellers, using their trading skills for a better way of life.

It was at the turn of the century 1903, that Crete changed the abandoned island into a leper colony where over 250 local people were brought by boat, never to return again to see their friends and family.

Walking up the stony path into the ruined City, we passed under the stone archway. Chris remarked that it was the same path those unfortunate people trod to start their new life inside the city. To briefly turn, and look over your shoulder for the last time, knowing that you will never see your family again. How daunting it must have been.

In 1913 Crete became part of Greece and many other patients were sent from the mainland. It was fast becoming much more organized as doctors and nursing staff, Caretakers and priests were living on Spinalonga. In the 1930's a modern building was constructed to enlarge the village, so each patient had more privacy in their own surroundings. Becoming very organized, despite their adversity, they farmed the land, fell in love, had children and died on the island.

A cure was found in due course, but not before many people had lost their battle for life. Empty burial chambers are still visible to one side of the circular path which runs round the small island. The colony closed in 1957, and to this day, it has remained empty and desolate with many buildings falling into ruin. Hundreds of visitors, like us, make the pilgrimage across by ferry each year, deeply interested and curious about its historical past.

It had a strange and empty feel to the place as we wandered around the ruined buildings and looking at the some of the small houses were the unfortunate people lived. The circular pathway gave a 360 degree view of the shore, and the large rocks directly below. In conversation, we said that some of these doomed people would have done this same walk many times, and looked over to the village of Elounda in pained frustration knowing they may never return, some having left their young children behind with other members of the family. The authorities did their best at the time by isolating sick people before it became an epidemic.

A certain young man of 21 years old caught leprosy and spent 20 years of his life on the island constantly campaigning for better conditions and forming a co-operative for better facilities. When a cure was found he was released and sent back into society; by then he would have been in his 40's!!

Glad to get onto the ferry boat again, and frightened of being left behind even for one night! We watched the island slowly become smaller as we sped back to Elounda for the evening. Back on dry land, the sun was still very hot as we said our next task was to find a nice room to stay in overnight. Earlier, we had seen a pretty taverna which rented rooms at the back of the building. After making initial enquiries, we followed a jolly local woman down the narrow path between their olive groves and up the steps to one of the pretty chalets.

'Oh! This is lovely, I remarked, sitting on one of the chairs on the terrace. Chris said that he thought we ought to have a rest on the beds out of the hot sun before getting showered and going out for dinner later that night. I had to agree, as the sun had been merciless all day, and with very little shade over on the island.

A few hours later after our siesta and a refreshing shower, we both dressed and took an evening walk along the promenade. A lot cooler and much more comfortable, we took our time in selecting a restaurant. The twinkling lights had been switched on around the harbor and in some of the restaurants as the owner invited hungry diners to come and eat. We chose a pretty restaurant which was on an elevated decking area, surrounded by a huge vista of tall palms and lush green plants, some with exotic jewel coloured flowers. All the tables were covered with white linen cloths, decorated with pretty candles and flowers. Tiny fairy lights were strewn along the outer perimeter, to highlight certain features within the decked area.

A smartly dressed waiter came out and smiling at us, presented the menu for the evening. As we ordered, Chris said that we would like a bottle of his best chilled white wine to compliment the meal. Other diners started joining us on the terracing later, lending a happy atmosphere to the evening. We both thought that we would enjoy eating the colourful fish platter for two people, as the waiter told us that all the fish was caught locally off the shore of Elounda.

A few minutes later, the waiter returned carrying the enormous platter in both hands, carefully placing it in the centre of the table.

'Wow! We both gasped in unison, 'just look at this! Nodding and smiling proudly, the waiter wished us 'Happy Eating'.

'Well, I said, looking at the platter, do we eat this or take a photograph of it?

Chris laughed, and said, I think we had better start eating it Patti, I am hungry.

The chef had dressed the outer part of the platter in a crispy mix of salad leaves and lily tomatoes, with twists of cucumber and lemon. A small black bream was placed on its belly in the very centre, with a large variety of King prawns, mussels, crab claws, B B Q'd sardines and squid; carefully arranged around the bream in a mouthwatering pattern.

We slowly savored the delicious seafood meal and enjoying the crisp and refreshing white wine, until we were so full we couldn't eat another morsel!

Next day we were up early and after a hot shower we paid the jolly owner at the taverna and left. We agreed to do a short detour and visit one of our old haunts from years back when we visited Agios Nicholias at Eastertime. It hadn't changed too much, although it appeared to be a lot busier and larger than we remembered it years ago; as then it was a sleepy fishing village and tourism had just started then. But we still enjoyed a few hours visiting and walking along the seafront to enjoy the cool breeze blowing from the sea.

CHAPTER 13
AMARI PLATAEU AND PATSOS GORGE

SEPTEMBER 2011

'Let's have a run out in the car today, I said to Chris, one bright sunny morning. We don't have any particular jobs to do today, and we should make the most of the days we have left here at Agia Triada'.

As I made breakfast, Chris opened our well used map to get some inspiration as to what region he would drive the car. Having recently bought a very interesting walking and sightseeing book, he browsed them both until breakfast was ready.

Eventually Chris said, 'why don't we just set off later and 'follow our nose' to see what adventures we can find?

'That's a good idea, I said munching my toast, we have had such a good time in previous days out, just being open minded and enjoying our day'.

It was slightly cooler weather now, after the oppressing heat of July and August. Climbing steadily up in our car over many narrow and bumpy roads we headed towards the Amari Plataeu. It was a much fresher breeze as we drove along with the windows open enjoying the countryside, with pungent smells of various herbs drifting in through the car window. Leaving the coastline behind, with the flat landscapes towards the sea, we turned towards the dramatic high face of craggy rocks, jutting upwards towards the azure blue sky.

Presently, I spotted the most beautiful little white washed church perched on the very top of a rounded hill; and persuading Chris to stop for a while we got out the car to walk up a very steep incline to the top. Ten minutes or so, we stopped to catch our breath, and look down into the valley below with several carefully tended vineyards set out in neat rows of terracing, positioned in such a way as to catch the constant sunshine. Further round, rows of olive trees, divided by numerous stone walls belonging to each farmer dominated that particular landscape.

At last, we reached the top and looked down at our car parked like a miniature matchbox toy, we were so very high up in the clouds.

'This is so beautiful I said, as I opened the little ironwork gate leading up to the church. Turning the huge key in the bleached wooden door, we stepped over the worn threshold, deeply curved with many pilgrims stepping on it as they entered. The creaking door swung slowly open and taking off our hats, we reverently stepped inside. Adjusting our eyes to the gloom, we sat down on one of the wooden pews to look round. The difference in temperatures was very noticeable, as the morning was still very warm, but inside the thick stone walls repelled the heat and it was very cool. Towards the Alter was an intricately carved dark wooden screen with iconic pictures of Saints; a mural of the Last Supper in the middle. A large and ornate brass candelabrum hung suspended by a large chain in the middle of the ceiling, with a myriad of cut glass shapes. The usual deep oval brass dish and stand was to the right of the a Alter. Filled with fine sand, and many thin candles nearby, they invite visitors to light one and say a prayer for a friend or loved one who has passed away.

Returning to the car some time later, we continued along the road and through the villages of Kare and Koksare. We use this road quite regularly to drive down to the south part of Crete and the Southern coastline.

'Hey! Just a minute, I said to Chris as we drove past a signpost which said 'Patsos Gorge'. That looks interesting, let's take a look.

As we walked down the dusty track, we saw a large well lit restaurant coming into view. Two sleepy donkeys, were saddled and waiting under the cool shade of a few large plane trees. At the end of the dusty path was the cavernous mouth of the Patsos Gorge. Walking through the double doors of the well kept restaurant, the staff was busy cleaning and mopping for the busy day ahead. It was still very early, and as we were the only ones there, we took our time looking round the grounds at the back of the building. To one side of the restaurant was a lovely waterfall running into a deep pool with a few ducks and geese either swimming around or sitting on the green bank over at the other side.

There were many purpose built wooden shelters in a large field with a varying number of small animals for visitors to come and see. There was a horse tethered up eating hay, and on the loose was a young bull!! The next thing we know, the young bull gets giddy and starts to charge around the field. I ran for safety, but as Chris has been use to dealing with cattle at his Father's abattoir a few years ago, horizontally held out his arms to stop the bullock running towards the restaurant and road.

'What are you now, a Matador? I said laughing.

At the far end of the animal farm we came to a pen with two large pigs, one sow and one boar. The boar was busy eating his breakfast from the 'leftovers' at the restaurant, the sow was laid flat on her side snoring and occasionally flicking her tail or ears to keep flies away.

Oh! Look at the boars face, Chris said laughing loudly; he's got a spaghetti moustache!!

True enough, he had a bright red 'moustache' over the top of his snout from the spaghetti sauce!!

We both roared with laughter as the boar looked quizzically at us in a way only pigs have. He eventually got fed up of us laughing at him and started eating the remains of his breakfast, and at the same time, nudging the sow on her bottom to get up and stop being lazy!!

Retracing our steps to the mouth of the gorge, we walked down the clear and well trodden path at the beginning of the gorge, as many do a short walk up to the lovely shrine further along, literally built into the rock face. Entering the gorge, it opened up like a huge cathedral, with magnificent coloured rock formation, deep waterfalls and pools.

The pretty little white washed shrine, Agios Antonios, the patron saint of 'lost articles' or patron saint of farmers, depending on which information you read! was so small, only two people could fit inside the chapel itself. Wedged on natural shelving in the white washed rock were several religious artifacts and icons, together with candles and incense burners. A constant stream of curious and reverent visitors trooped in and out of the tiny dirt floor shrine. We waited patiently until it was our turn, and removing our hats once again, stooped under the lintel of the doorway.

Inside, the church was lit by candles and on the tiny stone alters stood a dozen or more photographs of people who had died, left by friends or relatives expecting visitors to pray for them.

Leisurely climbing down the steps towards the clear shallow riverbed below, we continued further into the gorge along the stony path, becoming increasingly difficult as we progressed.

It's becoming even more impressive, I said, as we walk further down.' Leaving the constant stream of visitors behind and concentrating on where we put our feet. Watching for a moment, some little birds flying in and out of the natural holes in the rocks, and remarking on how impressive a cluster of stalagmites were over at the far side. The dirt path was replaced by a uneven stone one, but now, we were having to negotiate large previously fallen boulders as we continued further into the gorge. Climbing over some huge rocks and edging round others, we stopped now and then to look round us. A few knarled old trees lined our path, some hollowed out over time, struggling to stay alive with the diversity of weather. Exposed roots threatened to trip the unwary, twisted along the ground in a snake like fashion. Crossing the dry river bed one minute, to reveal a beautiful deep pool, and stare into the crystal clear water and to the very bottom revealing pretty coloured stones.

Striding ahead, Chris came first to the deep sided drop, and looking over the edge, he saw a thick chain which had been drilled and fastened to a huge boulder inviting the walker to grab hold of the chain and walk backwards down the rock.

'After you, I said smiling at Chris, as he shuffled up to the edge and grasping the chain.

'Now you, he shouted back at me smiling, 'take your time'

'Oh yes I will, I said nodding sagely and fear grabbing my stomach.

Gingerly I took my turn in shuffling forward, and trying not to look down (well I am frightened of heights!) took hold of the chain, and swung down to where Chris was waiting.

Phew! I'm glad that's over I remarked.

Continuing along, there was a little wooden bridge, so keen walkers could go over the fast flowing river to the other side and continue along the gorge. Fast waterfalls cascaded down the high jagged rocks into the little pools below, giving it the look of a fairy grotto. Looking into the water a few times to see if any fish lived there, I didn't spot any, just pond skaters and dragonflies with the sunlight occasionally catching their turquoise blue wings.

We didn't reach the end of the gorge that day, as the afternoon had turned into early evening and we needed to be sensible and reach civilization before long. Returning to the restaurant for refreshments and a rest, we got into conversation with an English guy, who lived and worked in Munich and was on holiday with his wife. Sharing a delicious meze with them, along with a cold drink for an hour, it rounded off our day's pleasure before we returned home for the night.

Chris parked the car near our villa, whilst I opened the front door to go inside. A little gecko had been sheltering from the hot sun saw his chance and scurried through the door and disappeared under the settee. My mouth dropped open in amazement, he was so quick!

A few minutes later, Chris came in and I told him what had happened. He said they are quite harmless, and will probably eat any bugs or mosquitoes which come into the villa.

We see our little pet every now and again, either in a corner of the room, trying to blend in with the brown tiles on the wall or high up near the ceiling, peering down at us as we sit on the settee. We think he lives in the fireplace as it is cold and dark, only coming out at night after we have gone to bed for his evening meal!!

CHAPTER 14
THE MYLI GORGE

SEPT. 2008. MAY 2010. AND SEPT. 2011

The pronunciation of Myli is Meelee, a corruption of Mill, and this gem of a place has a lot to offer for the adventurous, the seasoned walker, the enthusiastic and curious. The first thing which you notice as you carefully descend the steep path leading down to the gorge is how cool it soon becomes. Popular with tourists and shaded by the canopy of numerous trees and shrubs in the summer it is protected from the high winds and rain in the winter.

It was a busy working village up to the Venetian time, with many watermills turned by the natural springs and streams cascading down from the rock face high above.

The little church of Agios Antonios appears first, and is one of three here in the gorge. The churches are not locked, and one can sit and meditate in their cool stone interior. Outside, around the perimeter of the church is the original stone seating, and the local people would have their service outside in the summer months. A nearby natural spring supplies a cool drink for the thirsty traveler. The water channels now become apparent, and through the gorge you will see many ruined mills in the hillside, once fed by the stone aqueducts that drop from mill to mill. Descend further, you will start to see the beginning of derelict homes, and can actually visualize how they must have originally been in Minoan time. Restoration work is being systematically carried out to restore the village and mills.

Coming into view is the delightful taverna, with a cool and shady decking area overlooking the gorge entrance. It is a 'must' to sit awhile and gaze across at the magnificent side of the gorge with many natural caves. A pulley system is still in constant use, suspended across the gorge from the top road, to bring supplies in for the taverna. As you look over the fenced patio, many orange, and lemon trees along with pomegranate and fig trees originally planted many years ago, are now managed by the taverna owner, and used in the restaurant itself.

We have walked the gorge winter and summer. In the summer months, the footpaths and river beds are practically dry and its easy and pleasant walking. The winter presents a different story, as the rocks and boulders are slippery with algae from a constant flow of rainwater gushing down from the gorge sides. The taverna closes in the winter months, but you can gain access to the gorge at any time.

Crete has two months of constant heavy rain, January and February, so it is not advisable to walk in any of the gorges then.

As we steadily descend, following the almost goat track paths, twisting and turning and with rivulets of water running alongside us. Ivy and olive tree roots grow up through the limestone rock and threaten to trip the unobservant walker. Wild herbs are in abundance, and the warm damp atmosphere brings their pungent scent to your nostrils as we continued along. Buzzards circle overhead, making their familiar mewling noise, and ride the warm thermals. Look closely at the rock; you will see many stones and shells embedded with compression from the tectonic plates rising up from the sea millions of years ago.

We are coming to the lower stream bed, and crossing it, if you glance down at the crystal clear water, you can see lots of tiny coloured stones at the bottom. The temperature has dropped right down as we venture further along the steep descent. Lush green fauna and flora is evident and many stone water channels still run with the clear sweet mountain water.

Under a little archway, the remains of one of many derelict houses stand silent, some with the original walls surrounding their front garden. It was there, a lovely cool breeze blew across the gorge, and nearby one of the many natural springs; making it a convenient place to be when the houses were occupied. We were nearing the bottom of the gorge and leveling off, we crossed another clear stream and up the other side. There was a tyre nailed to a tree which said. 'Leave only your footprints'. We were getting near Adrian's place. We met our friend the very first time we walked the Myli Gorge, and he left us with lasting memories; being the only modern day person who we know lives in a cave. Yes! That's right; Adrian is an original hippy drop out and has lived in his conveniently cozy cave for over 20 years!

Born in New Zealand he has done a lot of travelling and had a very interesting life. I suggested to him that he should write his biography, he said, and that he will, one day. This particular day we met him, he was sat under the shade of a large tree painting some little rush seat chairs he had rescued from the local rubbish tip. Strung from the branches of trees surrounding his 'plot', were an assortment of quirky junk he had also brought back from the tip.

I have things to sell, he said, you can buy these chairs if you wish.

Well, thanks Adrian, but we don't need them right now!

I have books, do you like reading? Come into my home and I will show you.

Following him up the slope and onto the terrace, he had a crate of old musty books. I was looking into the mouth of the cave entrance by then, and really wanting to go in and take a look.

He saw me peering inside, and invited us both in to look round.

'You will have to excuse my untidiness; Socksie hasn't had chance to clean up today'.

He was pointing to a pretty little cat sat on a chair amidst many other items strewn around the cave. As we stooped at the entrance, the back wall of the cave was painted white with natural curves used as shelving to house some pictures and personal belongings. To our right, was his cot bed, unmade and in total disarray. A swept dirt floor was covered with various household items, and to the left, was his kitchen. He had a double burner which ran off Calor gas. A heating system was in place, with a big chimney running up through the roof of the cave. A little wooden table and chair was placed nearby and that was almost covered in pieces of stripped wood for his art work. He showed us some of his finished art work, and explained in detail of how he collects large vine roots from the gorge, dries and strips off the bark, then sanding them down to a smooth finish, he eventually varnishes them. I must say, they were really beautiful, but he was asking rather a lot of money for the finished work.

Returning outside again, we stood talking to him for an hour or more on various subjects, and then it was time to leave and make our way back.

The last time we came to Myli, we made a point of going to visit him, but he had already told us previously that he may be going to Holland over the winter to do some work. So we were not surprised to see his cave entrance closed up with a large piece of thick cardboard over the doorway and both windows. The surrounding area had been cleared of his art work in the trees. Chris estimated that he hadn't been there for at least six months or more with the untidy mess of many fallen leaves.

Oh! Look, I said, pointing further down the path, there is an arrow and a notice which says 'Banana Cantina'.

Let's go and take a look then, Chris replied.

On our approach, we saw several tables laid with paper cloths overlooking a small plantation of banana trees and bamboo canes lining a small stream from the gorge. On the other side of the path, the proprietor and his wife sat outside their little cantina watching four little kittens play together on a chair seat next to them.

Looking up, they motioned for us to sit down at one of the tables.

We both sat down and ordered a cool drink. She brought to us a small banana each off one of their trees, and then placed the drinks down. We commented on the size of the trees and noticed the huge clusters of unripe banana's waiting to ripen through the summer months. It was then the lady brought us a plate of local food as a meze, this is traditional with the small village taverna, as the Greek people always eat something when they sit down to have a drink. She gave us a plate of olives, sliced beef tomato, a small round rusk like bread, and fried courgette flowers! They appeared to be split in half, and dipped in batter then fried with herbs and sea salt. Absolutely delicious!! It was very pleasant sitting there after our meze, feeling the cool breeze blow gently down the gorge valley surrounded by the lush green vista.

We watched the kittens play with the fallen and blowing leaves for a while and tumbling over each other before excusing ourselves to re-trace our steps. The sun was at its hottest, as we walked slowly back and stopping now and then to catch our breath and rest. I saw something move out of the corner of my eye, and glancing down, I saw a tiny crab about the size of a 50p piece moving across the path, to take shelter beneath some rocks. It must have come from the stream bed, and the nearest one would be down a steep bank of ten feet, through a lot of undergrowth, to the stream below! Incredible!!

We continued past several natural open caves, with gates across or used to house a mule or goats by the local farmer. Many goats can be seen in daylight hours, wandering at will, feeding or taking shelter in the gorge bottom. One day when we were walking in this gorge, the taverna owner's dog joined us for a walk. He likes to chase the goats, but they seem to be too quick for him, and he eventually gives up the chase and returns to us. He escorted us all the way round, stopping now and then at places of interest just like the dog we had at Korinthos.

Climbing back into our hire car, tired but happy, we remarked what an interesting day's walking this had been.

CHAPTER 15
THE POROS GORGE

It was the most remarkable day for us when we did this walk! Or should I say situation.

I shall begin! Deciding the day before which walk we would do, prior preparations were made to pack the rucksack with a host of important items, and to rescue us from every situation, we thought!!

We woke to a very warm day, with climbing temperatures and clear blue skies. We set off from the villa very early so we could be in the gorge before the sun was at its hottest.

Always with plenty of cool bottled water in our rucksack, we were aiming to start the walk at a place called Agios Konstantinos. After a great deal of searching for the start of our walk at house number 153, the houses didn't run concurrently; we followed an E4 sign to walk alongside some mulberry and myrtle trees. Crossing the gorge along a stony path and up towards the little chapel, constantly following the vivid black and yellow wayfarer markings, although some were hard to find. Eventually, we passed a track which ran alongside the ruins of an abandoned village, pausing for a while to wander through their interesting remains. We are now on an impressive limestone terrain, and the tiny houses of Velonado come into view as we go onto the slope and the rounded mountain top. We find the wayfarers mark to indicate the start of the Poros Gorge, only to find the entrance was totally covered by a dense thicket of gorge and brambles, making it impossible to continue through!

By now, it was lunchtime, early afternoon, and the sun beat down on us from a cloudless sky offering no shelter whatsoever. Still very hot from the baking heat of the summer, the thick overgrown vegetation offered us no shelter on the day.

What do we do now, I asked Chris, it's impossible to get through these brambles. He stooped low, and inching forward, his rucksack giving some protection from the sharp thorns, tried to get through and see if it would open out into a clearing.

'I can't see a way forward, it's all dense brambles, and hasn't been walked in there for some time, he said.

There is only one option left for us now, we shall have to walk back down the road or go back the way we came'.

Talking at length, we both came to the decision to walk back along the road, not knowing how far we were from home!!

Pulling the map and compass out, we found a shady spot to try and get our bearings, taking a long pull on one of the large bottles of water.

'I never realized you could sweat so much just standing still, I said, studying the map with Chris. I feel like I have just been in a warm shower!

We started to walk back down the road, the sun reflecting off the road, dazzling us with its brightness. We had walked for over an hour, winding through the hillside with barren scrubland on each side of the road. A few grazing goats turned to watch us as we tramped along almost exhausted. Now and again, we would stop to replenish our thirst from the fast disappearing bottles of water.

Oh! Goodness me, I feel like one of the troops in the Foreign Legion.

We are committed now to carry on until we get our bearings.

Round and round the hillsides we went, up and then down, and still nothing in sight, only more scrub land and goats!

AH-HA!! Look over there, I said pointing in the distance, it's a Kafenion—hurray!!

Gathering our last bit of strength, we walked up the dusty track and thankfully sat down on two old wooden chairs in the shade.

They have a lot of refreshments here, I said to Chris. Look at all the crates stacked up over there.

Shortly afterwards, a pleasant middle aged lady came out from behind a flimsy curtain leading to the inside the room. With my limited Greek language, I asked her for two cold beers, please. She looked at me as though I had gone mad and shook her head. I said to Chris in a low voice, my Greek language cannot be so bad that she doesn't understand me. So I tried again, only said it slowly this time. Gabbling something in rapid Greek, she disappeared into the room again, shaking her head and shrugging her shoulders.

Well, I said, what do you make of that?

Her bizarre actions had rendered Chris speechless, and he just stared into the distance, not saying a word!

A few minutes later, from behind the curtained door came a pretty young girl of about 14 years old. She was typically Greek, with long dark curly hair and brown eyes which crinkled up at the corners when she smiled. 'Hello, she said, in perfect for English, 'please be our guests here, my Mother is just preparing some cool melon for you to eat'.

Being a typical English couple, we both said in unison, Oh! No, it's alright, we just need a cool drink and a rest' (beer was out of the question now, as the stacked crates in the corner contained her Papa's tomatoes ready for selling at market).

No! No, I insist, you are my guests today, she replied.

We resigned ourselves to the generous Greek hospitality, and returned a smile and thank you.

True to her word, a few minutes later, Georgia's mum came out with a tray of freshly prepared melon for us. Smiling broadly, she put it down on the table and encouraged us to eat. As we enjoyed the juicy red flesh of the large melon, Georgia asked us many questions about England and our lives there. Then she promptly told us about her school life and what exams she would be taking in the future with regard to her working life. She said that she would like to be either a lawyer or a school teacher in Athens, depending on her grades at school. We all sat together in the cool shade of their veranda, passing the time of day until the sun became cooler.

We heard a pickup truck coming down the dusty driveway, and jumping up she said her Papa was coming back from the fields. Previously telling us he grew tomatoes, and melons and made wine from his vineyard nearby; and also the famous Raki. Running to meet him, she introduces us to him, and shook our hand. Translating for us, as her Papa couldn't speak English, we apologized for intruding at his home. His face lit up as a big smile came to his rugged face, and waving his hand away, told Georgia to tell us that we were most welcome to sit and eat some melon with them.

Presently, Georgia's mum came out again carrying some more plates of melon. Some for her husband and some for us! I don't know if you can overdose on water melon, but as it is made up largely of water, it fills your stomach up.

'Eat my friend, eat' Papa said, waving his fork towards Chris, who was looking distinctly uncomfortable at the thought of having a few more kilos of melon!

Unable to tell him we both had eaten enough, but thought it would be rude; we picked up our forks, and gingerly poked at the large amount of melon left on the plates.

As I cleared the plate and replaced the fork, I suddenly had a horrible thought. What if the Mother keeps coming out with more and more melon, do we feel obliged to keep eating it until we burst all over the patio? Agh!! Perish the thought!! Pull yourself together girl, you've had too much sun.

Not to outstay our welcome, and time was marching on, we took our leave. Georgia got up and went in to her Mother, who, a few minutes later came out carrying three large bottles of iced water for us to take with us. Meanwhile, Papa brought a couple of carrier bags with his home grown beef tomatoes inside.

Georgia said, Papa would like you to take these back to your home.

There must have been about eight kilo of tomatoes in the bags, Poor Chris! He had just emptied his rucksack of two bottles of warm drinking water!! Once more, Chris was temporarily rendered speechless, and all he could do was to nod and smile, as to refuse such a kind and generous offer would have been unthinkable.

Lots of efghareesto (thank you) shaking hands, and waving were done, before setting off again to continue our journey. Ten minutes into the walking, I had successfully maneuvered one of the ice cold bottles of water up my back so that it rested on the waistband of my shorts! Oh! That is so nice, I said, turning round to see Chris puffing and panting up an incline with a rucksack full of tomatoes.

Tramping on for another three kilometers we seemed to be getting nearer to a village or at least a settlement of some kind. 'Are you hungry, Chris asked? "Starving" was the reply, all that melon has worn off and my stomach is rumbling something terrible'. As we approached the village, this time, there WAS a taverna waiting for us. A deep sigh of relief escaped from my lips as I watched Chris wrestle the heavy rucksack from his shoulders and drop it to the floor of the taverna.

This time, I shall order something long and cool and know I shall get what I ordered, Chris remarked. We both laughed at the funny situation we had got ourselves into, but also said that we would be extra careful in the future and avoid putting ourselves at risk.

Returning home to our villa, and settled once more, Chris reckoned we had done a 16 mile walk that day!!

CHAPTER 16
STRANGE AND FUNNY ANECDOTES IN CRETE

On our way out one day towards Heraklion, driving on the fast National Road, in the distance we see a line of light coloured material hanging on a thin wire fence surrounding farming land. As we drew level, we glanced across to see many newly washed garments hanging out to dry along the fence! and the farmers sheep grazing at the other side. Probably the farmer watched over his sheep and kept an eye on his washing at the same time?

*   *   *

When we first came to the Greek Island many years ago, the toilet arrangements were very basic to say the least! It wasn't unusual, in fact it was the norm, to enter a toilet block only to discover what was colourfully named as a 'ski jump' staring back at you from a broken tiled floor! For the uninitiated, it is a basic hole in the floor, usually tiled, and with raised metal foot pads on either side of the hole for you to squat down—or if you are lucky, being a man to 'aim and fire'. Unfortunately, if some of the men had missed their target and you were wearing a skirt, the whole business could get very messy!! Once you have neatly positioned yourself for a few moments, there really wasn't anything available to grab hold of and hoist yourself up again and quite often no toilet paper either!! Thank goodness, I say, when there was an upturn in the tourist industry and the Greek businesses installed modern cisterns with toilet paper. We haven't seen "ski jumps" for a long time now, neither in the towns or villages nor in remote mountain hamlets.

*   *   *

No matter where you go, or what you are doing, you will always see Cretan cats.

There is a huge population of feral and semi wild cats patrolling the streets in towns and villages, climbing into the large communal waste bins for scraps of food. Begging from the individual home owner as well as foraging for themselves in the olive groves and fields.

'You could take home a stray cat every day' a friend once remarked to me as we stopped to pet a particularly pretty little white cat with buff coloured markings; strolling through an orange grove near her home. 'It looks like she belongs to the local farmer, I replied as we passed by the semi derelict outbuildings with farm machinery laid to one side.

We have recently acquired a black and white male cat near our villa. He's friendly enough, I guess, and we think he belongs to someone in the village, but he has adopted us for extra support! The minute we open the patio door, he appears, purring and meowing for attention, and rubbing along our legs and ankles for a cuddle. That's all very well, but most of the ex-pats here are literally chewed to bits at certain times of year with mosquitoes and other biting insects, without having the added trouble of cat fleas to go with it! So the pet name for our communal cat began one morning when I was carrying my washing basket out to dry my 'smalls' in the hot morning sun. Appearing from behind the oleander bushes, out jumped the cat and started his daily routine of meowing and rubbing up along my legs.

Wobbling, whilst carrying the heavy basket, I shouted 'CLEAR-OFF!! Since then, all the residents living nearby have nicknamed him 'Clear-off'.

We think it's got quite a ring to it, don't you?

*   *   *

We love and respect the way the Greek people conducts their lives around the Greek Orthodox churches. The beautiful shrines and churches are built to honour the Saints of that particular church, and come together as a family to worship. It is quite normal to see the young men going about their business of the day, pass by a church and slow down either in their car or motorbike to cross themselves. This always reminds us of our childhood in the 1950's—attending church regularly and in particular, to celebrate Mothers Day, and other holy festivals. We were expected to walk up to the top of the church on Mothering Sunday and receive a posy of silk violets surrounded with several dark green leaves from our vicar to present to our Mother on return.

Similarly, the Cretan church attendee's have holy festivals at certain times of year to celebrate the coming of Easter, naming days of Saints and anniversaries. The Greek people love to celebrate and have a day off to join in the fun. Each town and village has their own particular saint or saints, and could have two or three small churches within a short distance. On the naming day of a particular church, e.g. Agios Eleni, all the local people will visit and take part in the service to celebrate on that day, leaving it empty the 364 remaining days of the year.

*   *   *

Completing a walk we did one day a couple of years ago and on return, we decided to deviate from the good road and head up to a village we had yet to see. The tiny village of Mirthios hangs suspended from the nearby Myli Gorge, and the Amari plateau. Stopping in the car park, at the very centre of the village, we walked across to the taverna and up some steps onto a broad terrace. Chairs and tables were placed outside, and fresh vegetables were neatly stacked in boxes against the wall. But the door of the taverna was firmly closed.

Chris remarked that there wasn't anyone around, and we should leave.

Ignoring him (again!) I knocked on the door, and a moment later it was opened wide to reveal a smiling old lady. Her plump body waddled out onto the veranda, and pulling a chair out invited me to sit down.

Ordering two light refreshments, she returned to inside the taverna and brought back out with her two cool beers and two plates with assorted mezethes, which consisted of some small bread rusks (a hard, break your tooth filling) some goat cheese, beef tomatoes, sliced and black olives. Thanking her, we sat back to enjoy our drink and meze, and look out over the lovely Amari plains.

Not long after that, she emerged again bringing out a large bowl of pomegranates' and then sitting down on a rickety chair nearby, we watched, fascinated, as she proceeded to open the pomegranates with a sharp knife, to later turn them inside out; and collect the juicy segmented interior along with the others. A few minutes lapsed, and looking up at us, she struggled to her feet and came over to give us the little dish she had collected. A warm smile spread over her face, making her eyes twinkle as I kindly thanked her. She was later joined by her husband on the veranda, who nodded an acknowledgement to us, and sat down near his wife.

We had eaten everything she had put in front of us, and glancing round the veranda, our eyes fell on a very large metal hook, suspended from the high wooden ceiling above. In conversation, we agreed that it was probably a hook to hoist a goat up by the back legs and cut its throat. As it was unlikely they would be able to understand us, Chris said loudly, 'that is probably what they do if tourists refuse to pay'. With that, the old guy turned round and started laughing, and pointing up to the hook, proceeded to make a slicing motion across his throat! We all gave up to a good hearty laugh!!!

*   *   *

As we drove along a quiet mountain road one day a very bedraggled and scruffy old man suddenly jumped out from one of the olive groves, which ran alongside the road. Beckoning us to slow down and stop, and without further ado, he opened the back door of the car and got in. We were both quite stunned for a moment, and turning round, we see him looking back at us, his grubby face widening into a toothy grin. No razor had touched his face for a while, and he badly needed a good haircut.

Muttering something in a low growl, he waved his hand for Chris to set off again. Now the day was quite warm! And as we proceeded, a pungent smell started to emanate from the back seat. Still constantly chattering away to himself, he grinned at me once or twice as I looked over my shoulder to see what he was doing. Chris discretely opened the car window, as, by now, the smell was becoming unbearable. Then suddenly, without further warning, the old man gave Chris a sharp tap on his shoulder for him to stop the car. Ambling over to yet another olive grove, he slumped down under the shade of an olive tree and closed his eyes.

*   *   *

We were very lucky to be here in Rethymnon to see the wonderful parade through the town centre, marking Oxi Day (No Day) it falls on 28th October every year.

It is a much celebrated festival all over Greece, consisting of parades and folk dancing commemorating the Prime Minister saying NO to Mussolini's ultimatum in 1940.

Last year we parked on the marina car park in time to watch all the attractions go by. Many Cretan people had turned out to watch, some with young children hoisted up onto Papa's shoulders to get a better view. Visitors like us, mingled around in the crowds, and all were looking forward to the start of the parade.

We heard the brass band starting up and in marching time in all their uniforms, they lead the parade of teenage girls and boys dressed in National costume. The steady procession came continuously with the children from various schools in the prefecture of Rethymnon, and at the front representing each school, a young person held their flag on a long pole, each having the name and number of the school. The equivalent of cubs, scouts and brownies and girl guides followed on, representing the World Wide movement for Rethymnon town. The Boys Brigade marched past, the older men at the front who would instruct and train the younger ones behind. My favourites were the little ones—boys and girls, dressed in the National costumes of Crete, looking so cute my eyes filled up with tears as they saw their parents along the road and waved.

Lots of pictures were taken both from their parents and some guys from the local newspaper, who knelt at the very side of the road to get better pictures.

The lovely procession continued for some time, all representing their club, school or pastime until they all marched down the street and disappeared further along the town. At the front of the town hall, local dignitaries were each giving a short speech followed by appreciative clapping. Later on, as we strolled through the old Venetian town, many Greek families were heading for their favourite restaurant to eat, drink and celebrate as only they know how.

*   *   *

CHAPTER 17
DITTANY HERB (Origanum Dictamnus) and The Diktamos Gorge

The Dittany herb flower is quite short stemmed, growing close to the ground in many bleak and remote areas of the mountains. It clings to the side of cliff edges where even grazing goats find difficult to reach. Consequently, it flowers in abundance and self seeds every year; covering large areas of mountainous region with swathes of pretty yellow/orange colour.

A delicate and hardy flower, long ago doctors believed it could cure lots of illnesses. It was also used to help women with pain when giving birth. Such was its fabled power that many ancient writers believed it worked its magic on all open wounds.

The goddess of love, Aphrodite is thought to have come to Crete and gather dittany to use as a medicine, and so the belief evolved that this pretty little herb was a plant of love! And to also encourage the feeling of love! Over the following years a tiny sprig would be exchanged between lovers as a token of affection.

One day, a few years ago whilst we were out walking in the mountains, we came across two crusty old men standing talking in a small village hamlet. Greetings were exchanged with light conversation. One of the old guys had a tiny sprig of dittany behind his ear, reaching for it, he gave it to me along with a toothy grin! Pointing to Chris, he gesticulated, 'this from him to you'. We did not know the lovely story regarding the herb at that time, it was much later we were told about it.

'Is there a link to the name? Origanum Dictamnus and the Dictamos Gorge, I don't know! I would like to think there is, as they are both very beautiful! Maybe it grows in the mountains surrounding the gorge?

8th OCTOBER 2011

The Dictamus Gorge nestles slightly inland from the coastline almost opposite the beautiful Souda Bay. A cloudy but warm day saw us up and out early to do a full days walking. Passing through the pretty fishing village of Georgiapoli where many colourful boats are tied up along the harbor walls. The narrow road is framed by several large plane trees continuously shedding their barks throughout the year. We noticed two or three fishermen down by the little marina, busily weighing the 'catch of the day' on a large and rusting weighing scale to sell later on at one of the attractive restaurants in the village.

Driving through the sleepy village of Vrisses, just waking to supply the locals with breakfast, either on the terrace of their home, or sitting in a sheltered spot outside one of the taverna's, and enjoying the morning sunshine.

As we climbed up on a steady helter-skelter like road, into the foot of the mountains, with continuous breathtaking views we wound in and out of some more little dwelling places pausing to take one or two photographs. As the sun climbed higher in the sky, industrious housewives in the villages were busy outside their homes to wash their front veranda and steps and start their daily cleaning routine.

'Oh! No! I exclaimed, 'there's Michael Winner!! An elderly guy on a twist and go motorbike was coming toward us. The doppelganger had a mop of white hair, with his face was crinkled up against the sun.

'Oh yes, Chris replied, he does look a bit like him, Michael Winner must have bought a summer residence here in Samonas village then?

Presently, we come to a well 'shot at' road sign, which looked like it had been regularly used as target practice with a bazooka or a Kalashnikov rifle! Many road signs in the mountain regions are like this, some are splattered with tiny pellet shot; others have a five centimeter hole in them!!

At last, we arrive at Dictamus Gorge, and still have plenty of time to do our walk for the day. Our walks book tells us that it is a three hour walk to reach the far end of the gorge, but we are open minded regarding the terrain and climate; and sometimes abandon the walk to return to safety. It also states that it is a good walk in the hot summer months as there would be plenty of shade.

Donning our walking boots, and hats, Chris hoisted the rucksack up onto his back and then 'we were off!!

We appeared to have the gorge to ourselves as we started out on our walk, instantly sheltered by the large oak and cedar trees, with a few reedy oleanders outgrown in strength, trying to reach the leafy canopy above. We dropped down, almost right away and onto the dry riverbed which was completed covered with fallen autumn leaves. They continually drifted down onto our heads as we passed under the high arc of mature trees. The warm sun peeped through now and then, throwing dappled sunlight and then shade into the gorge. It was cool and comfortable as we walked, even though it was approaching midday.

Further along, the gorge started revealing its hidden treasures from the outside world as the huge sides of the gorge walls showed layered colour striations, and several deep caves. Blues, red and green seams fell in thick layers, sometimes horizontal and sometimes vertical, rising high to the very tops of the gorge walls. Scrubby trees clung onto the narrow rock shelves, battered with the yearly winds and hot baking sun. The dry stony riverbed path gave way to larger rocks and boulders as we ventured further into the gorge, spasmodically marked with a red wayfarer dot to re-assure us that we were on a permitted path.

We were now coming to a series of giant 'gorgonzola cheese' rocks and boulders, with tiny rock plants growing out of some of the holes. Many rocks and boulders had tumbled down from the sides of the gorge years before, and lay where they fell in careless piles at the bottom.

The walk became a continuous scramble now and thankfully we had our leather walking boots on to lend support to our feet and ankles. Pushing on further, in our enthusiasm to see what was around the 'next corner', and stopping now and then to admire the magnificent gorge interior. Continual evidence of flotsam and jetsam was wedged between the rocks and boulders from previous years when the winter floods had rushed in from the sea and largely covered the gorge interior. Many large and heavy tree branches had been caught up in the clefts.

'Here is an old rusty milk churn, I shouted over to Chris, 'and there is a large lorry tyre as well'. We both stopped to look at the remains of a red car, which must have been hurled into the sea and washed down the gorge at some point, with many dents and holes in the metal body. We marveled at how the mighty force of water came rushing and tumbling through the gorge every year.

Resting for a while to take a drink of water and look about us, Chris pointed out the groups of hard compressed rock and mud with lots of beach pebbles inside them. The island was formed with the movement of 'tectonic plates', causing a mighty thrust from the earth's crust and forcing rocks, stone, shells and marine life up to the surface, compressed through many millions of years to eventually form the island of Crete.

'Wow! I said, taking a closer look, it almost looks like someone has painted pale blue and pastel coloured circles on the rocks, worn smooth with all the constant pounding from the elements.

You could smell them before you could see them, the pungent smell of a large herd of goats grazing in the shade of the trees and nibbling at a succulent morsel. The goat bells became louder, the nearer we came, echoing round the high sided walls of the gorge. Standing back against a deep cleft in the side of the gorge, we allowed them to pass us by with their young kids so as not to scare them. Some paused to stand and stare back at us quizzically for a moment before joining the others which had wandered further down the gorge to graze again. There must have been about forty or more goats and kids, some with magnificently large and curled horns rising vertically from their head and with cute goatee beards!! One large goat stood and stared at us, as he perched high above on a large boulder; he wasn't fazed by our presence.

Moving on again, ourselves and the goats, as by then, some had nimbly climbed a lot higher to avoid us completely and walked along a narrow shelving, bleating loudly to encourage their kid to follow, their thick and hardy goatskin ranged from a pale creamy colour and mid brown through to black.

We had been walking and scrambling for over two hours and I started feeling tired as the effects of constant climbing over some boulders had started making my thighs ache badly. Taking a rest against a particularly large boulder, we had another drink and looked about us. Only the sound of the soft wind rustling through the remaining leaves on the trees could be heard. Tilting my head up to the warmth of the sun, I closed my eyes to enjoy the heat on my face.

Rested and refreshed, Chris said he thought it advisable to turn back the way we had come. On the return journey, it was no less exciting and interesting than when we had set off earlier in the day.

Leading the way, Chris shouted, 'Hey! Look at this!

As I caught him up he was pointing to a very large boulder, which had been constantly battered by continuous rainfall and rushing water year on year. It had literally been 'carved out' into a very splendid stone seat!!

'Oh! I like this, I said grinning, and carefully lowering my derriere down, I wriggled about for extra comfort. 'It would look brilliant in our garden back home, I said, looking up at Chris.

'Does the seat fit? He replied laughing, 'I don't think I can get it into my rucksack today'.

'With an amused grin, I replied, Oh! Yeh! The seat fits—just about, ha ha . . .'.

Further down the gorge, we came across a 'table', attached horizontally across the mouth of a small natural cave in the gorge wall.

'Now that looks like a troglodyte could have had a very desirable residence here many years ago, I said laughing. 'It almost looks purpose built, doesn't it—quite perfect in fact'. 'If the river bed didn't flood, a caveman could live here quite comfortably on nuts and berries, the occasional goat, fresh drinking water nearby and a delightful stone table to eat off!!

'Come on Chris remarked, don't get carried away with it all'.

Other thoughtful walkers had built small cairns (small pile of stone in a pyramid shape) to help other walkers along the permitted path when the 'red dot' had temporarily disappeared. Chris thoughtfully pointed out that the cairns must have been done this year, because of the annual floods which would have washed them away.

As we took our boots off and replaced them with lighter shoes, we watched a farmer and his wife vigorously shaking one of their walnut trees, and see them tumble down to the grass below. To be eaten locally along with fresh figs and oranges, as well as many other locally grown produce.

Returning to Georgiapoli village we decided to 'round off' the day and have a light meal and refreshments. We parked the car in the shade of an old plane tree which ran alongside the reed marshes framing the inlet of water from the sea. Marsh birds had gathered in and amongst the thick reeds obscuring them from sight when nesting and feeding.

'Shall we come another day when it is less windy and the sea isn't so choppy, so we can walk out on the causeway to the little church at the far end? I said.

We were perched on the centre of the little bridge which ran over the narrow inlet, watching sixty four geese (Chris counted them) being continually bullied by one lone swan! The swan in question must have been either mad or bad, as he was in the process of rounding up and attacking any poor goose that had broken away from the rest. Then he would paddle furiously to get up some speed and with his head forward in a charge position, aim his large beak at the unfortunate goose!! We watched his performance for over ten minutes until he had successfully corralled them all into the narrow inlet opposite our parked car.

'He doesn't seem to realize that there are 64 of them, Chris remarked laughing. I have never seen that before, it's like he's on some kind of mission'.

'There he goes again, I pointed at the swan, his wings spread out and flapping furiously he did another head charge at the large group of geese.

'Too much sun I think, Chris countered, the crazy bird thinks he is a collie dog, rounding a large flock of sheep!!

CHAPTER 18
ANOPOLI AND ARADHENA GORGE

14th OCTOBER 2011

Talking to our Belgian neighbours one afternoon by the swimming pool, I asked them where they had been recently. Carmen explained that they had done a gorge walk which was a favourite of theirs, and have gone back several times to enjoy the peace and tranquility of the gorge. With her mention of 'ruined village' and a 'very high steel bridge across the gorge'—we were hooked!!

After dinner that evening, Chris got our map of Crete out, and re-traced her directions with his finger to eventually arrive at the village of Anopoli.

After an early start next morning, we set out towards the National Road to turn onto a secondary road towards Hora Sfakion, which was quite a direct route. The sun was still very warm, even though it was now October, and alongside our picnic, we carried two chilled bottles of drinking water in our icepack bag.

En route to the pretty village of Vrisses, the magnificent Lefka Ori (White Mountains) rise up in the distance, covered in snow from

December to June the following year, rising to a couple of metres short of the highest point of the Psiloritis mountain range.

Passing through a series of tiny hamlet, where time has stood still, and still functions today as they did many years ago. I feel at peace with the world on days like today, as we bob along in our car, the suns warmth through the window, soft winds and bright blue skies, in October!!—could one wish for more?

Travelling in companiable silence for a while, I remark on how beautiful the small forests of pine trees are nestling in the mountainside. Suddenly, as Chris took a steep right hand bend, he had to swerve to avoid two chunky white hessian bags in the middle of the road which must have come off the back of a lorry. Pulling to one side of the road, he ran back and cautiously dragged them to one side, so as to avoid a serious accident.

'Are you okay, I said as he climbed back into the car. 'What was in the bags'.

'I don't know, he replied, but I think the lorry driver will realize they are gone, and return to pick them up'.

'Almost there now I said, pointing to the road sign for Hora Sfakion, its only 35 km'. We continued to climb, up and up on a helter-skelter road round the mountains, cautiously passing large rocks which had been dislodged from above the road, either by heavy rain or an over ambitious goat!!

Small herds of goats were grazing at the side of the road, with some actually sitting down in the road itself to enjoy the constant heat from the suns warmth!! A few minutes later, we saw an old farmer putting something down for them to eat.

'Ah! There is the white hessian bags, Chris remarked; 'he must be putting a food supplement down for them'.

'No wonder the goats sit in the road then, I said, 'it's because they have got use to the farmer feeding them at the side of the road'.

'Chris! I need the loo' I said, can we stop somewhere, preferably a toilet block and not behind a large bush!!

'We are near Imbros now, Chris replied, I wouldn't mind finding out about the gorge walk at Imbros whilst we are here, so we can do it another day'.

We had our morning coffee in a newly built restaurant overlooking Imbros Gorge, at the same time; Chris made enquiries regarding the walk.

'There's the sea! Chris remarked, and stopping the car we looked down below at the microscopic resort of Hora Sfakion.

'That is what you would call an alluvial plain, Chris said. I asked him to explain what that meant. He said, 'it's debris which is brought down by several rivers to form a plain or flat land, from way up above in the mountains'. 'It is often fertile, but on this occasion, it is unlikely, as the whole of the landscape round us is very rocky. Maybe millions of years ago, the mountains would have come right down to the very edge of the sea'. 'This particular landscape is quite unique, having two or three gorges relatively next to each other'.

The downward spiraling road takes us through the seaside resort, quiet and peaceful once more, now the holiday makers have gone home. A few gaily painted apartments and hotels support a shingly beach. With the pretty bay and lagoon, a ferry boat is tied up alongside a few little fishing boats.

Leaving them all behind, we are now heading towards our final destination of the village of Anopolis and the gorge of Aradhena nearby. We are on a relatively new road now which has been hewn through the side of a mountain. Jagged 'plates' rise up in a semi horizontal fashion as if it were the under belly of the mountain itself! Blasted away in an attempt to widen the road, we pass through three or four tunnels, with goats sheltering inside the tunnel for comfort out of the hot sun.

Briefly passing through a small hamlet, we agree that it must be very hard to make a living there, as we do not see any fertile land whatsoever, only an immense amount of limestone rocks littering the landscape.

Eventually, we arrive at the village of Anopolis and park in the square. A monument has been centrally placed to mark the execution of a brave local man who dared to stand up against the Turkish invasion. I made some tentative enquiries regarding the whereabouts of the gorge, to a young woman who was coming out of school holding her son's hand. She pointed down the narrow lane, and said that it was approximately two kilometers to the head of the gorge.

It was the amazing view of the high suspension bridge which caught our attention as we parked nearby. Carmen had told me that her husband Jan had driven over the bridge, and scared the wits out of her as it made a horrible drumming noise!

Changing our shoes to walking boots, we gathered up the rucksack, and quickly had a cool drink of water before setting off to walk over the bridge. Taking some photographs of the ruined village over to the other side of the gorge, and of the magnificent steel bridge which was built by a local businessman in 1986, who was born and brought up in Ayios Ioannis, the tiny village further down on the opposite side of the gorge, so they would have permanent access to the outside world and stop the village from 'dying'. Unlike the now ruined and abandoned village opposite, where it was abandoned because they had to walk along a meandering goat track to come down one side of the gorge and up the other side to gain access to the outside world! Amazing eh? What must it have been like when the winter floods came? They would have been totally cut off until the following spring when the water receded.

Tentatively stepping onto the bridge, my stomach started doing the familiar butterfly dance, churning and doing a series of back flips! I suffer with vertigo and am I really frightened of heights, and the height of this bridge down to the bottom of the gorge measures 130 metres! How anyone can actually pay to bungee jump off the bridge in the summer months is beyond me; they would have to pay ME to do it!! The broad wooden planks, like railway sleepers, lay horizontally across the bridge, with narrow gaps in between so you could see through them, and down to the stony gorge below. Chris was half way across, busily taking photographs of the gorge walls and caves totally unperturbed by its height. Determined to conquer my fear, at least temporarily, I steeled myself, and yelping now and again, did a sort of pirouette across the now wobbling boards to the other side; taking a not so graceful leap (a bit like an elephant doing a par du deaux) in the air over to the other side!!

'Phew! I said, staggering towards Chris, 'my legs have gone all wobbly, and I feel funny!

He shot me a look, which without words, said it all!!

Recovering enough, we walked towards the partially restored village where one or two, we later found out, have moved back into the houses. Further along, we saw a crumbling building which could well have been the local bakers and instrumental in crushing grapes or olives at one time; as in the far corner, was the most beautiful old winding press, rusting now, amidst the interior dereliction; but still held in place by a very old broad beam of wood presumably olive wood. In horizontal fashion, it would have originally been wedged between the low ceiling of the dwelling and the top of the iron press. Nearby, lay a huge quern, a massive grinding stone, probably used for grinding wheat to help make the village bread. We stood for a moment, inside one of the remaining houses, no roof now only a crossway of rotting olive wood beams which would have held the roof in place. The remains of the fireplace were still visible, together with an inglenook carved in the stone wall where the dry goods of salt and flour would be stored to avoid dampness.

Ambling over broken stone walls which would once have been built around a small garden growing the household vegetables, we opened a thin wire gate to keep a small herd of goats out of the gorge entrance. We could hear some noisy chatter coming from inside one of the occupied houses, along with aromatic cooking smells.

Moving down towards the gorge head, we notice a little white washed church and reading the information board; it is a Byzantine 14th century church, with an unusual pepper pot dome and named Mihail Arhangelos. Trying the well worn circular handle, it was locked against us; we later discovered that several items had been taken from inside the church!! Hard to believe!!

We pass some more evidence of a ruined town, which is believed to be an unexcavated Greco-Roman town called Araden, whose stone was instrumental in building the old church.

Carefully picking our way down the steep winding incline, we pause to look over to the other side of the gorge and see the original goat track path where the villagers would have once used. Dangerously steep and with the absence of any handrails, it is seldom used only by a few daring walkers and stray goats! We could smell various wild herbs growing along the side of the steep path as we slowly descended, their perfumed scent made stronger by the warm sunshine.

Ten minutes later, we reached the very bottom of the gorge and the arid riverbed; the yawning chasm stretching long and wide, inviting us to walk its length. Turning right, by a well placed cairn of stones, we eagerly walked towards the steel bridge, set high over the gorge. Chris had already decided before setting off that morning it will be 'a look and see day' as time was marching on and we needed to get back down the mountain before darkness fell at 6-30 p.m. Too many hazards, falling stones, goats in the road, made a lot worse by a series of hairpin bends and narrow roads.

We remarked on the lack of trees here in this particular gorge, as when we have walked in others, there has been a huge canopy of trees sheltering their interiors. However, we had the added advantage of being able to see the gorge walls in all their splendid details—vast striations of varying coloured rock formation, many natural large caves and diverse structures of the gorge walls.

'Hey! Chris, come quick', I said excitedly, as I had been watching where I walked over some of the large rocks. Seeing something move sharply out of the corner of my eye, I turned to see a thin snake about 18 inches long slither between rocks and olive tree roots. Its distinctive markings were black and white alternate oblong shapes.

'Too late, I said pointing to the cleft in the rock; it's disappeared down there behind the olive roots'.

Huge boulders of limestone rock rise up in our path as we continue along and admire the stalagmites and stalactites suspended from one of the large caves above our heads. Now the walls of the gorge had distinctive coloured stripes of pale blue to reddish brown and grey making it resemble a painting by a giant artist.

Chris remarked on the grisly remains of dead goats along our track, which must have either fallen from the ravines above edging forward to eat a tasty morsel just out of reach, or alternatively, been swept away in the winter floods.

Sparse and undernourished trees hang in an outward direction from the rock face, continually battered by wind, sun and rain they continue to survive, only to be nibbled at by some daring goat, which will climb to the very edge in order to reach out.

Incredible 'larval' looking rock is in abundance, which resembles the description of 'moon rock'. We seem to be in a time warp, nothing has changed here in thousands of years! Quite remarkable!! Crunching slowly along on the pile of deep riverbed stones, we pause to eventually look up, directly vertical to view the underbelly of the steel bridge. One or two cars, like a child's miniature, drive over the bridge, making a noisy thrumming sound as the wooden planks reverberate against the metal.

'Oh! I AM GLAD we didn't drive over the bridge, I don't think my heart would have stood it, I said putting my hands over my ears and wincing.

Directly below the bridge and near to where we stood, were large amounts of steel cable still coiled from when the bridge was constructed. Sitting on a huge boulder and resting for a while before returning back to the car, we gaze round in silence, to take one last look at such a remarkable place, lost in the mists of time, it is now, as it must have been thousands of years ago; nothing has changed it, and hopefully, nor will it in the future.

CHAPTER 19
GOURVERNETOU AND KATHOLIKO MONASTRIES

8th NOVEMBER 2011

Writing my notes up on a previously exciting day out, I was half listening to Chris reading aloud some information regarding a Monastery over the other side of Chania.

'We have already been there,' I said, as I stopped writing for a moment.

No! This walk is further on, and it says it has magnificently high cliff top scenery, with a fabulous walk down to a ruined Monastery'.

'That sounds interesting, although I am not sure about the bit that says 'high cliff top scenery' remembering the steel bridge at Aradhena Gorge recently.

Our clock alarm went off at 7-00 a.m. and jumping out of bed, we both hastily got ourselves ready for the full day ahead.

Driving along the National Road in the same direction as Suda Bay and Chania airport, the sun was just peeping out as we passed over Petres Bridge. One of my favourite places to collect driftwood for the fire, with its oval bay and clean white sand; now deserted after the holiday season had finished. I love the way the clusters of dark jagged rock further round the bay, rise up in interesting rock spires from the clear deep blue waters of the Mediterranean. Drawing Chris attention to remark on a couple of cormorants perched on the spiraling rocks, with their large black wings open in a cape like fashion, to dry them in the warm morning sunshine.

Young plane trees reveal their autumn beauty of red and golden leaves glinting in the sunlight. Tall pines and mature cypress' line the road as we motor along towards our destination. Deep red swathes of Virginia creeper grow out from the rocks giving a curtained appearance, with many oleander trees still producing their deep red and purple flowers.

A few large fish farms are strung out in Suda Bay to our right as we circle the mountainous roads, whilst further along we see the old fortress built on a large promontory overlooking the Bay itself. Originally built as a look out during various invasions, it is now used as part of the military base. Passing the airport sign, we continue along to follow the many road signs which lead to several different Monasteries.

Driving along the straight road leading to Agia Triada Monastery framed by a series of tall straight trees, their lower trunks painted with a white wash giving an air of importance; the reality is the white paint is to deter some form of 'pest' from killing the trees.

Passing by the impressive Agia Triada Monastery with its ochre coloured walls, and neat and well tended vineyards nearby, we pass some large expanses of more olive groves and vineyards until we reach some huge stony outcrops of land.

'Well! This looks like the place that time forgot', I said, glancing out of the car window on both sides of the road. 'Most of the Monasteries here in Crete seem to be built in relatively inaccessible places, either perched so high up a mountain it takes you all day to get there; or along here, at the ends of the earth.'

Eventually, we started coming to a much softer terrain, with undulating hills covered in vast amounts of deep purple heather, interspersed with a large quantity of beehives; side by side in several long rows.

'Those hives must belong to the monks, I said, as well as the olive groves and vineyards'. 'This road seems to have been widened and remade quite recently too, it must have been quite impassible in the rainy months at one time'.

'They won't be using donkeys any more Patti, Chris said laughing, they will have a heavy duty four wheel drive now to get them about on the roads'.

As we approached the Monastery of Gouvernetou, and impressive but simple square structure in similar colour to Agia Triada Monastery but some years older. The final path gave way to a clustered rocky outcrop with wild olive trees bent and twisted from the constant harsh winds blowing up the gorge from the sea. Parking a little way back from the Monastery gates, to respect their wishes; we realized that the Monastery was closed to visitors earlier that day, and would open after Evensong much later in the day when we had gone back home.

'That's a shame, I remarked as Chris opened our walks book to the appropriate page.

'It doesn't really matter, there is much more to see today, with St John the Hermit's cave and the ruins of the old Monastery of Katholiko; we can always return another day.

After putting on our now shabby and unpolished walking boots resulting from the constant dust thrown up whilst out walking on the dry paths and tracks, we followed the large sign to start our walk. At the beginning of the carefully laid stone path we could walk side by side, but it soon narrowed dramatically and we were now walking in single file; relatively safe having been cemented in part to avoid rockslide. The rocky terrain of the path consisted mainly of limestone and sandstone boulder ground down to give maximum grip. Keeping a watchful eye on where we were walking, in case a protruding edge caused a bad fall; we were delighted to see a large amount of delicate rock plants growing out from the tiny fissures in the rocks. Some were of similar appearance to a pale lilac winter aconite, their tiny petals growing closely to the ground to protect from harsh weather conditions. Others were a larger version of our marsh marigold in size and shape, their vivid yellow petals in stark contrast against the creamy stone path. Similarly looking dandelion flowers grew in some small areas further along, their faces turned up to greet the warm sunshine.

Chris had now taken the lead to watch ahead of any hazards which may occur. Pausing for a moment to look at the vertiginous ridge of the ravine, as the path slowly wound its way down in a series of corkscrew bends so that one got the feeling of walking suspended along the ridge top. The views were truly breathtaking as we looked over the deep ravine below, and across to some ruins half way up the other side.

'It looks like somebody has lived over there at one time', I said, the building remains are still largely intact and one could make out the circular corral that would once have held either sheep or goats. The stony remains of a retaining wall were still visible amongst the overgrowth of wild thorny scrub.

'That looks like a lime kiln,' Chris remarked pointing over towards a cluster of derelict buildings.

We saw a few more old lime kilns, some with light brown domed roofs still intact. Several caves were very visible, used by early Christians as the large cave of St John the Hermit; which we would see further along our path.

Our leather boots creaked and strained as we carefully picked our way over the gradually descending path, with the added luxury of stone steps. We had both noticed, as the sun reached its zenith; lots of little gecko's scurried out of our path to disappear back into the tiny natural holes in the limestone rocks. Most of them had a brown upper body with long thin green tails!

'It's like gecko-ghetto, Chris remarked laughing, I've never seen so many all at once'.

Pausing for a moment to catch our breath and admire the view, the crystal blue waters were now apparent through the parted ravine and down towards the sea. Many years ago, there was a tiny natural harbor where some visible remains of a boat can be seen. At this time, marauding pirates used the port to constantly raid the Katholiko Monastery which was eventually abandoned over 300 years ago.

We were arriving at the metal gate to enter Holy ground and the substantial cave of St John the Hermit, believed to have lived and died here in constant Christian worship. As we enter, the wide mouth of the cave opens up to show some very beautiful stalagmites and stalactites from centuries of constant dripping water inside the cave. But at the very centre of the cave is an unbelievably large stalagmite, very broad and about seven foot high; unfortunately painted white!!

Very old and worn steps lead up to a large bathing tank which was used long ago for baptisms. Believed to have been an important Minoan shrine, it is dedicated to the Goddess Artemis. As we didn't have a strongly lit torch with us, we could just make out that the cave went on much further, carefully treading on the fine sandy interior floor, we could see a narrow passageway right at the very back of the cave.

Quite near to the cave entrance is an old shrine built into the rock face, similar to others we have seen recently. Stooping to enter, we are faced with purposely cut stone shelves displaying icons of Jesus, Mary and the Saints. Holy relics are nailed to the stone walls and an incense burner hangs suspended at the far end. Over the other side of this fenced interior, and partially fallen away down the steep ravine, are some ruined remains of stone buildings where once must have been a small Christian community.

Closing the gate behind us, we venture forth once more to descend the last few minutes on the rockier and much steeper path to the very bottom. It was well worth the strenuous effort as stretching out before us was the entrance to the ruined village and the abandoned Monastery of Katholiko. The path was very narrow at this point, and with the aid of the smooth and rounded rocks to our left, we swung round to find a wider path further along. Pausing to look at several small niches purposefully cut out in the rock, which would have held lit candles for pilgrims to find their way.

'Oh! Wow!! I said, standing gazing down towards the Monastery through a delightfully ornate stone archway, intricately carved with scroll and leaves, still very visible.

'This is amazing, Chris gasped, as he walked down the worn steps and towards the archway to take a photograph.

I panned round taking in the part ruined cells where the monks would have lived, and a series of restored outbuildings. The famous 'bridge to nowhere' mentioned in our walks book, ran across to the other side of the gorge and abruptly stopped at some tumbled rocks and further dereliction of some other part of the Monastery.

I joined Chris inside the Monastery, and looking up I could see the lovely arched stone roof, and where it eventually met the actual rock face. Wooden benches and some individual seats were neatly stacked up in one corner of the large room. A very large wooden cross and brassware took centre stage on the alter itself, and drawn across were two clean cotton curtains.

'This all looks very clean and well cared for, Chris remarked, the monks must come down here regularly to clean and hold services.

We walked round for a while, looking inside the doorways of the recently renovated cells, and the deep stone ledges where the monks would have rested after toiling at their work, and praying regularly in the Monastery church. Presently, I noticed a sloping footpath leading down through a narrow doorway at the side of the bridge. Calling to Chris to come and take a look, he noticed that there were the remains of another doorway at the far end towards the ruins. In deep discussion, we thought it must have been where the monks would have stored their dry goods such as hay, straw, flour etc through the winter months.

'They must have been very self-sufficient here, I said, it's a great pity the pirates kept raiding the Monastery'.

Reluctantly, we came away and started to climb back up the steep stone path to reach the top and our car. As always, when we have had such a remarkable day as today, we lapse into complete silence as we re-live our experiences and marvel at the day's event. This was one of those days!!!

CHAPTER 20
AND FINALLY . . . .

Our adventure holiday is coming to an end; as we are due to fly out of

Heraklion airport to Manchester, England on 22nd November, 2011; and enjoy a quiet Christmas and New Year at our other home on the Fylde

Coast in Lancashire.

2nd January, 2012

I have almost finished writing this book, and hope you have enjoyed reading it as much as I have thoroughly enjoyed writing about our many experiences whilst touring in the motor home.

However, it isn't the end of our holiday adventures as we are already planning the next trip through Europe.

In the spring of 2012 we will be packing the motor home and driving down to our villa in Crete. This time we will be using the Dover/Calais crossing and motoring through France towards the South Coast. Maybe stopping off for a few days in Paris, to do some sightseeing. Then on towards Marseille and Monaco, and over the Alps into Italy; to follow the coastline which runs alongside Genoa.

We would like to spend a few days on a campsite near Venice, and possibly take in a musical recital this time. Then ferry across to mainland Greece and spend some time touring in the Peloponnese.

If it all goes well, I will be returning to write my second book!!

Printed by Amazon Italia Logistica S.r.l.
Torrazza Piemonte (TO), Italy

15241001R00128